LEARNING
TO DO
WHAT *Jesus* DID

HOW TO PRAY
FOR PHYSICAL,
EMOTIONAL AND
SPIRITUAL HEALING

By Michael Evans
With Wholeness Ministries

Published by
Archer-Ellison Publishing Company
P.O. Box 950696
Lake Mary, Florida 32746
Phone: (800) 449-4095
Fax: (800) 366-4086

In cooperation with:
Wholeness Ministries
P.O. Box 80503
Bakersfield, California 93380
Phone: (661) 833-2920
Fax: (661) 833-2934
E-Mail: mevans@wholeness.org
www.wholeness.org

Cover design by Bookcovers.com

Printed in the United States of America

ISBN 978-1-57472-232-1

All Scripture quotations, except where specifically noted in this publication, are from the Holy Bible, New International Version, Copyright 1973, 1978, International Bible Society, used by permission of Zondervan Bible Publishers.

SCHEDULING A WHOLENESS
MINISTRIES TRAINING CONFERENCE

To receive additional information, discuss
financial arrangements or set a conference date,
please contact Rev. Mike Evans.

WHOLENESS MINISTRIES
P.O. Box 80503, Bakersfield, CA 93380
Phone: 661-833-2920
E-mail: mevans@wholeness.org

Acknowledgments

The writing of this training manual has been a team effort from the start. I wish to thank my wife Jane, for her encouragement and support which never wavered, and my children Joshua, Jordan and Jenny, for allowing me to follow God's calling on my life. Specifically for the writing of this manual, I am indebted to the following people whom God brought around me to contribute to this task: Bob Vibe, Elizabeth Sheldon, Wanda Danforth, Elaine Gaddie, Jane Evans and Jana Deem. For the countless hours spent formatting and editing, I am indebted to Bill Deem and Carla Kliever. My deepest thanks also go to Allen and Kimberly D'Angelo for their part in bringing about the professional quality of this book, for their work on its cover and their prayers and encouragement in seeing this project to its completion; and to the wonderful team at Twin Oaks Retreat Center for their unselfish giving of time and materials. Much gratitude also goes to the current Wholeness Ministries Task Force: Rick Dickard, Myra Lucas, Jana Deem, Travis Kirkendoll and Jane Evans for their support and willingness to keep after it until we completed what all of us knew to be a work of God. In addition, I wish to thank the one to whom the Lord gave the burden for this task, who carried it on her heart and saw it through to completion. I know she would want to remain anonymous, but God knows her name, and to her I will be eternally grateful.

I also extend my thanks to my "buddy" Howard Kliever who always believed in me and lifted me up when I was down. Sincere gratitude goes to our intercessors, those who serve on prayer teams and our supporters who are willing to back this ministry, and to my friends Bill and Lynne Wright who believe in what we are doing and have been there from the very beginning. I am especially indebted to Elsie Reed for her mentoring, encouragement, and prayers over the years. She taught me what it means to minister the love of Jesus in a gentle yet firm way to the oppressed and beaten down. I also want to thank John Lavender, who insisted I attend John Wimber's "Signs & Wonders" healing conference which changed my life; Wesley Brown, who made allowance for Wholeness Ministries to be birthed at Bakersfield Christian Life Center/First Baptist Church; Jeff Sampson, who "saw" the call of God on my life and constantly encouraged me to "do the stuff", always pushing me beyond where I was comfortable going; Pastors James Ranger and David Goh for whose encouragement, support and friendship I am deeply grateful; Stan Franklin, who, in my early years as a Christian, slowly drew me back into the church and became my pastor and dear friend; and Gary Clark and Joe Atkinson for their encouragement and prayers.

Lastly, the man whom I believe has had the biggest impact on my life is my friend Francis MacNutt. He is a man who believed in me, encouraged me, brought me alongside him and mentored me. Only time will tell how significant these years of friendship with him have been. In him I have had the privilege of seeing a man of God live out humility, compassion, gentleness and strength.

My heartfelt gratitude to each and every one of you.

Mike Evans

Table of Contents

Introduction to Wholeness Ministries

Wholeness Ministries was first established in 1989 under the covering of Bakersfield Christian Life Center/First Baptist Church, Bakersfield, California, with Mike Evans, as the pastor responsible for the ministry. This ministry was God's gracious response to the prayers of many people over the preceding years for a model that could be used to train and equip lay people to do the ministry of Jesus through the local church. In the early years there was little material available on how to organize and bring about the establishment of prayer teams in a local church; so began the development of this training manual by the Wholeness Ministries Task Force. This was a group of people which at that time included Mike Evans, Wanda Danforth, Liz Sheldon and Bob Vibe. The first edition of this manual was published in 1992 and has proved to be a valuable resource to churches throughout the United States and in several foreign countries.

In July 1994, Wholeness Ministries was incorporated and established as a non-profit organization under the leadership of Mike Evans. What is written here is the result of a process God has been taking us through over the last several years, combined with much of the material from the first edition. Additional resources have been added to help in training prayer teams, as well as material that will assist ministry leadership with some of the administrative functions. Much of what is included here is the result of our own experiences in doing "hands on" ministry, material from books we have read, training seminars we have attended, and extensive time on our knees before God. The manual you have in your hands is the second edition. The writing team for this edition included Mike Evans, Jane Evans, Elaine Gaddie and Jana Deem, with prayer support from a small army of faithful intercessors.

The purpose of this material is to give you a model with practical guidelines for establishing prayer teams that can function in your church. We know that all of this material may not be applicable to your church; however, it will provide you with a practical, working model with which you can begin. We extend to you this note of caution as you begin to read this manual: Each church is unique. Be cautious in applying this material in a "wholesale" fashion to your situation. Please try to avoid expecting to see the things mentioned in this manual occur for you in exactly the same manner as it has occurred for us. As you go before God and truly seek what He wants to do in your situation, we know that He will be faithful to reveal His plans for your local church body and we pray that this manual will be of help to you.

We believe that our role is to equip believers, through proclamation and demonstration, to do what God has called us to do. Let us emphasize that Wholeness Ministries does not have all the answers. We are still in the process of learning. We are learning how to pray, how to listen, how to discern what God is saying, how to see what God is doing, how to rightly divide His Word and how to "do His ministry." We believe that God is moving through Wholeness Ministries to equip people to fulfill His mandate of Luke 4:18-19.

"The Spirit of the Lord is on me, because He has anointed me to preach good news to the poor. He has sent me to proclaim freedom for the prisoners and recovery of sight for the blind, to release the oppressed, to proclaim the year of the Lord's favor."Luke 4:18-19

Section 1: Biblical Basis for Healing Ministry

The Centrality of Healing in Jesus' Ministry

Bringing healing and wholeness on many levels in people's lives was absolutely central to the ministry of Jesus Christ when He was physically present on earth. There are 41 distinct instances of Jesus bringing physical and/or mental and emotional healing in the Gospels, including the following:

- Man with unclean spirit (Mark 1:23-27)
- Man with Leprosy (Matthew 8:2-3)
- Man with withered hand (Luke 6:6-10)
- Widow's son raised (Luke 7:11-15)
- Gadarenes Demoniac (Matthew 8:28-33)

As Jesus was preparing His disciples for His departure He specifically instructed them to continue to do what He had done on earth.

> *I tell you the truth, anyone who has faith in me will do what I have been doing. He will do even greater things than these, because I am going to the Father. John 14:12*

Healing through the Prayers of God's People

One of the primary avenues by which God chooses to bring healing is through the prayers of His people. Built on our understanding of the priesthood of all believers (1 Peter 2:5, 9) and that all believers are gifted by the Holy Spirit (1 Corinthians 12:4-7) and called to use the gifts in ministry, our calling includes equipping the people of God (Ephesians 4:11-12) to participate actively and responsibly in becoming a community that truly ministers wholeness and hope. Some examples of God healing through the prayers of His people include these instances:

- The early believers prayed God would heal people (Acts 4:30).
- Many were healed by the Apostles' ministry (Acts 5:12,15-16).
- Phillip had a ministry of deliverance and healing. When they saw what he did they paid attention to what he said. (Acts 8:6-7).
- Ananias was sent to bring healing to Saul (Acts 9:17-18).
- Paul prayed for healing (Acts 28:8).
- Peter prayed for the paralytic, Aeneas (Acts 9:32-34)

> *Therefore confess your sins to each other and pray for each other so that you may be healed. The prayer of a righteous man is powerful and effective.*
> *James 5:16*

Varied Gifts Are Used to Bring God's Wholeness

Jesus' ministry of bringing healing and wholeness needs to be central to the church's ministry and must continue through His people today. In the power of the Spirit, we want to contribute to spiritual, emotional, psychological and physical wholeness (1 Thessalonians 5:23). The ministry of healing can take place in many settings. God also uses a variety of skills and spiritual gifts to help bring that about, as He did in the Early Church.

I have prayed for people in Cathedrals, warehouses, open fields, homes, airplanes, hospitals and prisons. I never cease to be amazed at the variety of places and ways that God heals. In the late 90's on my first trip to Budapest, Hungary I was part of a street ministry with Adam Balogh, our missionary in Hungary. We were meeting in the town square across from the train station. This is a busy place because at quitting time thousands of people pass through here on their way to catch a train home. After some preaching we began to pray for a number of people and watched as God healed and delivered them. At one point as I was standing there in the town square when it hit me what an amazing God we have. Here I was, out on the street, preaching the Gospel and praying for the sick in a country that had only been free from Communist rule for seven years. Earlier we would have been arrested and possibly shot. In addition, we were across the street from the main train station from which Hitler had shipped over 300,000 Jews to the death camps. God not only brought down the walls of Communism but allowed us to go out into the marketplace and proclaim and demonstrate His Good News!

Some examples of this variety follow:
- Disciples given authority and direction (Matthew 10:1,8)
- The Twelve sent (Mark 3:13-19)
- The Seventy sent (Luke 10:1-24)
- Jesus gives the power to bind and loose (Matthew 16:19)
- Peter heals crippled beggar (Acts 3:6-8)
- Apostles heal many (Acts 5:12-16)
- Eutychus raised from the dead by Paul (Acts 20:10-12)
- Call for the Elders to pray and anoint with oil (James 5:13-15)
- Peter raises Tabitha (Acts 9:40)

There is a danger that we come to expect God to heal in a certain way if we say just the right words or if we anoint the individual with oil or lay hands on them or perform some other ritual. We can close ourselves off to the infinite variety of ways God may choose to heal. We may be offended by how an individual prays for healing (loud, boisterous, demanding.) We may be turned off by their ministry style, dress, or belief. We must come to accept that God uses an infinite variety of people and ways to accomplish His healing.

I attended a healing seminar where I witnessed that when people were being prayed for, the hands of some of those praying were trembling. Not having seen this before, I quickly concluded that it really was not biblical and was probably attributable to the emotion of the moment. I relayed this comment to a brother who was likewise convinced that this behavior was questionable and we concluded that it was obviously not for us as we were reasonable men not easily overcome with such emotions. The next evening we were praying for a woman standing by us who had asked for prayer for scoliosis in her back. As I put my hand near her back, guess what started trembling? Not only that, but my hand also moved up and down her back as we watched in amazement the spinal column move and shift so that shortly she was completely healed and standing upright. Needless to say my friend was quite puzzled by my "emotional" behavior and I was embarrassed and perplexed that this had happened. That evening as I was talking with God I asked him this question: "Why did you do that to me?" He said, quite clearly, "Michael do not ever make fun of how I may choose to heal people." Needless to say I quickly got the point.

Different Dimensions of Healing

Just as it did in Jesus' ministry, we understand that healing may have different dimensions. God sometimes heals sovereignly without prayer, sometimes as a result of general prayer, and sometimes as a result of specific prayer targeting particular needs. It is important for us to remember that we are not responsible for healing. Our responsibility is to be obedient and pray; God is responsible for the healing.

> *I planted the seed, Apollos watered it, but God made it grow. So neither he who plants nor he who waters is anything, but only God, who makes things grow. 1 Corinthians 3:6-7*

- One dimension is **Spiritual Healing (Repentance)** for personal sin (Acts 2:28, 3:19, 1 John 1:9). This repentance can be both for salvation and/or sins we have committed as believers. Scripture clearly tells us that all mankind is born into sin. Unless we repent and accept Jesus as our Lord and Savior we will spend eternity separated from God.

- Another dimension is **Physical Healing** (Luke 4:38-40; Mark 1:40-42). This may be instantaneous, or it may require continual prayer over a period of time, sometimes called "soaking prayer." If we are led to pray for physical healing, God answers our requests in a variety of ways. There may be full healing, an improvement, or no improvement that we can see. Sometimes sickness is "sickness unto death," which for the Christian is the "ultimate healing." Healing is God's work, so we acknowledge that we stand before much that is mystery.

- A third dimension is **Inner Healing**, dealing with the past (Luke 19:1-10). Inner healing, which is concerned with the healing of past hurts, involves vividly recalling and honestly facing those times of hurt and asking Jesus to bring healing to those wounds. We believe that inner healing is valid for the Christian ministry today. Our understanding of Jesus' mandate in Luke 4:18-19, is to free us from the evil which burdens us today, take the memories of our past and heal the wounds that have resulted from them and which still affect our lives in the present. This appears to be what happened when Jesus accompanied Cleopas and his friend on the road to Emmaus, listened to their heartache and questions, and helped them find understanding from Scripture and transformed their gloom into joy by His presence (Luke 24:13-35).

- Another dimension is **Deliverance** from demonic oppression (Mark 1:23-27, 32-34; 5:1-20). The demonic realm is very active in today's world. The church is still called to minister the liberating power of Jesus from all kinds of bondage. Though we often avoid those who need deliverance due to our feelings of inadequacy or insecurity, we need to recognize and accept the responsibility of the call to minister total healing and wholeness, part of which will include the ministry of deliverance. This ministry demands careful preparation (often with fasting) and should be done by a prayer team of two or more people, who understand this type of spiritual warfare (Eph. 6:10-18).

In Wholeness Ministries we build upon the model of our Lord Jesus Himself and the experiences of the Early Church in the book of Acts, while at the same time being open to all of the insights that God can give us into the human condition and the needs of people. These insights must be consistent with what God has revealed in Scripture.

When you begin to aggressively move into a ministry of healing prayer, be prepared for opposition, for it will come. You will hear such things as; "the gifts are no longer relevant, this is not scriptural, it is New Age." You must not give up, but continually seek what God would have you do and persevere in your calling.

Section: 2 The Role of Faith and Authority

When a new believer becomes a new creation in Christ, he is born of the Spirit of God. In this realm of God's Spirit abide "faith, hope and love", according to 1 Corinthians 13:13. Faith is a spiritual substance and when we become a Christian, God gives us a measure of faith. A key area we will look at in this section is the role that faith plays in the ministry of healing.

Faith

Many of the books on healing stress the role that faith plays in the healing ministry. One widely quoted scripture is found in Mark 11:22-24.

> *Have faith in God . . . I tell you the truth, if anyone says to this mountain, go, throw yourself into the sea, and does not doubt in his heart but believes that what he says will happen, it will be done for him. Therefore I tell you, whatever you ask for in prayer, believe that you have received it, and it will be yours; Mark 11:22-24*

If we consider this scripture alone, one can easily see how many Christians believe that faith without doubting will give them whatever they ask for. This belief has brought many Christians disappointment and confusion. We are asked to have a faith in which there is no doubt or hesitation. Although it is easy for us to accept that God forgives sin, it is difficult to believe, in faith that God heals because we can readily see that healing does not always occur. Our aim in this brief study of faith is to recognize that the role of faith is important, but not the single ingredient necessary for healing or effective prayers.

There are generally four basic attitudes toward healing with regard to faith that are discussed by Francis MacNutt in his book Healing:

- Healing is man's responsibility.
- Healing is possible, but extraordinary.
- Healing is ordinary and normal, but does not always take place. (This is our position.)
- Healing always takes place if there is faith.[1]

Faith Defined

> *Hebrews 11:1-3 contains one of the best and most often used definitions of faith found anywhere:*

> *Now faith is the substance of things hoped for, the evidence of things not seen. For by it the elders obtained a good testimony. By faith we understand that the worlds were framed by the word of God, so that the things which are seen were not made of things which are visible. Hebrews 11:1-3 (NKJV)*

"Faith is the substance of things hoped for . . . "

If we have faith in God, we know that we can trust Him and that He will meet our every need as He has promised His children. This faith produces hope. This hope is not in the things that we see, but hope is based on the evidence of the unseen world, the Spiritual realm, where God's Kingdom rules and reigns over all, both visible and invisible.

> All of our hopes are based on faith and can be expected to be fulfilled only according to the faithfulness of the one in whom we have put our faith. We may hope to become wealthy because we bought a lottery ticket. We may hope that our complexion will be beautiful because we use a certain brand of soap. We may hope to become successful or famous because of faith in ourselves, but all of these hopes are based on the reliability of the source of faith and may disappoint us. Hope built on faith in God and His word will produce optimism and confidence toward life that can't be acquired any other way, because it is based on God's faithfulness.

> In Romans 4:17-21, the example is given of faith and hope working together in the life of Abraham, who was given the child of promise through his elderly wife Sarah.

- Abraham was strong in faith, believing that God would perform His Word.

- Abraham's faith produced supernatural hope, against hope in the natural realm.

Without Faith

> *Without faith it is impossible to please God . . .Hebrews 11:6a*

No amount of "religiosity" can gain God's favor. He cares about how loving you are. He is concerned with our inner motives, desiring that our primary motivation is faith working through love. When we love God, we find our love for others causing us to act in faith. Our faith is demonstrated by actions of love.

Remember:
It is our faith in Jesus that gives us life! Our faith can be costly!

I was invited to a maximum security prison to share with the inmates how to pray for the sick. When I teach I always like to have some "hands on" ministry by praying for someone and letting them see the power of God to heal. I remember well the words of the chaplain who invited me to come. He said, "When you come here you better be serious about what you believe. If you are phony in any way these inmates will get up and walk out. They can tell whether you really believe what you are talking about." If you were there as an inmate and claimed to be a Christian, though they may not agree with you, if you don't live what you claim to believe it could cost you your life! They would jump you and beat you and in some cases kill you.

The Source of Faith

We are all given a measure of faith. Romans 10:17 adds that . . . "faith comes from hearing the message, and the message is heard through the word of Christ." Faith grows in our heart as we put the Word in our heart.

The new creation of God's Spirit in us feeds on the Word of God, and Christians grow and manifest the works of the kingdom as they grow in knowledge and their personal relationship with God.

In I Samuel 17 is the familiar story of David and Goliath. When David first arrives on the scene as a young shepherd boy he is surprised that Goliath is taunting and ridiculing the armies of Israel and that rather than attacking they are shrinking back in terror. David says in verse 26, "…who is this uncircumcised Philistine, that he should taunt the armies of the living God?" In other words, who does he think he is, doesn't he understand who we are? David's relationship with God was such that he was sure of his identity, and could not believe that the army would shrink back in fear of this loud mouthed Philistine.

Faith Developed Through Testing

Our faith not only grows, it is developed and tested. In fact, James (1:2-3) tells us to count it all joy when our faith is tested because this will produce patient endurance or perseverance. This is the ability to "hang in there," to stand fast and overcome while giving thanks to God. The result of endurance and patience is revealed in verse 4 (Amplified Bible): "Let endurance and steadfastness and patience have full play and do a thorough work, so that you may be perfectly and fully developed (with no defects), lacking in nothing."

Wholeness Ministries began in 1989 when I was an associate pastor on staff of a large church in California. In 1994 the Lord took me aside and made it very clear to me that He was going to bring about some major changes in my life. I was sitting by a river near my home and God and I were having a conversation about my future. At one point I asked him, "God, are you saying you want me to resign from my position with the church, giving up my salary and security?" He said, "Yes, you can no longer do there what I want you to do." I said, "But God, you don't understand. I have kids, a house payment, bills, etc." He said, "What's the problem?" I replied, "WHAT'S THE PROBLEM! What about the bills, food, etc.?" He interrupted me and said, "Michael, what's the problem?"

Suddenly the lights came on and I realized that I was, after all, talking to the God of the universe! So what's the problem? God was saying to me, "Michael, I know what your needs are. I am asking you to do something you've never done before. Are you going to trust me in this?"

Hebrews 6:12 reveals that "through faith and patience we inherit the promises of God." We cannot fully understand faith without understanding the role of patience and perseverance.

The faith which is given to us also has the capacity to increase.

An example would be in in discerning God's voice. When I am praying for someone, God often puts a word, thought or picture into my mind. Many of these words related to medical conditions that I did not know existed. God would put a word into my mind like diverticulitis and I would not have a clue as to what that meant. I would take a risk and speak these words. As I speak them and they are confirmed my faith increases so that I am more willing to take risks and speak out what I believe God is saying to me, even if I am not sure what it means. Once in a healing service I heard the word "septum." I said, " I believe there is someone here dealing with a problem with the septum," hoping that was a real word. When I said the word someone stood up and said, "That is exactly what I am dealing with!" As I have taken these risks my faith has increased.

Paul told the Corinthians in his second letter to them (2 Corinthians 10:15) that he had a hope that when their faith increased, his ministry to them would be able to increase.

> *So as we learn of God's faithfulness, grace and mercy, and as we trust in him, we will find our faith growing.*

In 2 Thessalonians 1:3, Paul gave thanks to God because the Thessalonians' faith was growing and their love toward each other was abounding.

Faith and Perseverance
Is it faith to continue to ask God for healing or anything else you need?

> *Keep on asking and it will be given you; keep on seeking and you will find; keep on knocking and the door will be opened to you. For everyone who keeps on asking receives, and he who keeps on seeking finds, and to him who keeps on knocking it will be opened. Matthew 7:7-8*

An example of faith and perseverance is what we refer to as "soaking prayer." This is similar to an individual with a serious illness such as cancer who goes to the doctor for weekly treatments. Soaking prayer is continuing to pray for a specific ailment over a long period of time until complete healing occurs. It is literally "soaking" a person in prayer and God's love for an extended block of hours, days or weeks.

Scriptural Examples of Faith's Role in Healing

Belief Encouraged and Rewarded:
- Matthew 8:5-10, The Roman centurion
- Matthew 9:20-22, The woman with the issue of blood

Act of Faith Required:
- John 9:1-41, Blind man told to wash in the Pool of Siloam
- Luke 17:11-19, Ten lepers told to go show themselves to the priests
- Matthew 9:27-30, Two blind men

Faith of Friends:
- Mark 2:2-12, Paralyzed man lowered through roof by friends

Healing without the Person's Request:
- Mark 1:23-27, Man with an unclean spirit healed in the synagogue
- Luke 6:6-10, Man with a withered hand healed on the Sabbath

Healing with No Mention of Faith:
- Acts 3:1-8, Peter heals the crippled beggar
- Mark 1:30-31, Peter's mother-in-law
- Mark 7:32-37, Deaf and mute man

Unbelief or Lack of Faith May Hinder Healing:
- Luke 8:54, Jesus put out those who did not believe

Healing by Others:
- Luke 9:1-6, The Twelve sent out
- Luke 10:1-16, The seventy sent forth
- Acts 3 and 5: 12-16, Healing by the disciples

There is No Pattern

It should be evident after examining Biblical examples of healing that there is no pattern. From this observation of Scripture, we can submit a basic principle that is applicable in praying for healing:

- **There is no universal method or experience that can be applied to all cases.**
  Before praying for a person, pray for guidance from the Lord. In the beginning it is not unusual to spend more time talking, listening and building faith before actually praying. Sometimes healing cannot proceed until deliverance, confession, forgiveness or change of attitude occurs.

Praying in Faith

How shall we pray in faith then?

1. Turn to God in complete trust. He knows what is best and He loves us more than anyone else. He has the power to accomplish whatever we need.

2. Accept our doubts about our own inadequacy.
These are normal. The truth is, in our own power, we are inadequate. By understanding our authority in Jesus we can pray for and expect healing. It is Jesus who is sufficient to meet every need.

Such confidence as this is ours through Christ before God. Not that we are competent to claim anything for ourselves, but our competence comes from God. He has made us competent as ministers of a new covenant—not of the letter but of the Spirit; for the letter kills, but the Spirit gives life.2 Corinthians 3:4-6

3. **Let our faith result in action.** Pray for the sick when our guidance in prayer indicates this. We must pray in an atmosphere of love for the one for whom we are praying.

4. **Freely ask God to meet needs.** He can easily meet the needs of the person for whom you are praying but avoid telling Him when or how to do it. If a person seems not to be healed after we pray, we shouldn't be anxious. Oftentimes healing prayer begins a process that takes time to complete.

Remember :

Faith is important for healing but it is not the single ingredient necessary for healing or effective prayers. We have the easy part——to pray with as much faith as we have. God will do His part. We can count on that. Our faith lies in the obedience of praying for the sick, despite our doubts.

The Authority of the Believer

In addition to comprehending the role of faith, the prayer team members need to have an understanding of the authority that has been given to us in Jesus Christ. For most of my life I did not understand that this same authority was resident within me. We will explore the nature of the believer's authority and how we have been given authority to heal. We are indebted to John Wimber for his excellent teaching on this subject. The following material is adapted from a teaching given by John Wimber at a Healing '87 Conference.

1.   What is the Difference between Authority and Power?

- Power (Dunamis) is MIGHT or ABILITY, both inherent and spontaneous. This is the word which is the root of our word dynamite. It is an explosive word. It is often used for the word "miracle". (Mark 6:2)

- Authority(Exousia) is the FREEDOM and RIGHT to act. It is the freedom to exercise that power. (Matthew 28:18-19)
  Let's say you are a person going to law school. At some point you graduate and receive your diploma. At that time you have the ability (power) to practice as a lawyer. However you cannot practice as a lawyer until you pass the Bar Exam which then gives you the (authority) which is the freedom and right to act and exercise the power.

2.   Only God has Absolute Authority. He is Almighty.
  Yours, O Lord, is the greatness and the power and the glory and the majesty and the splendor, for everything in heaven and earth is yours. Yours, O Lord, is the kingdom; you are exalted as head over all.1 Chronicles 29:11

- We understand that all authority is ultimately delegated from God (Luke 1:51-52)

- Delegated authority denotes power that is linked to a position or commission: i.e., who we are in Christ, our mandate (Luke 4:18,19). In Matthew 10:1, 28:18-19 there is clearly a commission. Jesus' authority was delegated to the disciples. Because of our position (Romans 8:16-17) as co-heirs with Christ we are also recipients of this delegated authority. When the President of the United States sends an ambassador to a foreign country, that ambassador has delegated authority. He represents the President of the United States and has the power of that office behind him.

- In the spiritual realm, position and authority are to be understood in relational terms; i.e., we are called to be servants. Matthew 20:25-26 teaches that true spiritual authority is a relationship of service. What we do must be done with a servant's heart.

The Nature of Authority

"We have been given a truly awesome privilege and responsibility. In the Scripture the concept of authority is closely connected with the concept of power. In the New Testament, both power and authority flow from the work of Christ; first as He employs it and then as He empowers His followers to do His works. Jesus received His power from the Holy Spirit, and His authority from maintaining His intimacy with the Father. It is the God-given right to receive and use God's power that flows from the indwelling Holy Spirit.[2]

We Have Been Given the Authority to Heal

Through creation, God gave man a relationship, identity and position with Himself. This gave man authority (Genesis 1:26,27). In this passages from Genesis God said, "Let us make man in our image, in our likeness and let them rule..." We were created to rule over all of creation. Through deception and sin, man lost his position and authority; Satan became the prince, ruler and god of this world (2 Corinthians 4:4). Jesus was sent as a man to re-establish God's authority over the earth by disarming all powers and principalities and saving man from their authority through His death and resurrection.

It is important to understand that although Jesus was God, scripture clearly shows that He did not operate in His divinity while here on earth, but operated in His humanity, empowered by the Holy Spirit. Even when He was tempted by Satan in Luke 4, or in the Garden of Gethsemane when He could have called on twelve legions of angels, He humbled Himself in obedience to God the Father. Understanding this helps John 5:19 make sense.

> *Jesus gave them this answer: "I tell you the truth, the Son can do nothing by himself; he can do only what he sees his Father doing, because whatever the Father does the Son also does." John 5:19*

This is important for us in that we have available to us the same empowering that Jesus had. We are not divine, we are not Jesus, but we can do what Jesus did by submitting ourselves to the power and control of the Holy Spirit.

What Our Authority is Not

1. First of all, the basis of our authority is our position in Christ and not our feelings. We may not always feel authoritative but our feelings are not good indicators of truth.

Once while ministering in Budapest, Hungary it was very late in the evening and I had prayed for a lot of people. I was tired and wanted to go home to rest. I did not feel like praying anymore for anyone. I prayed for the last person in line and headed for the door. Just as my host and I reached the open door a young girl touched my shoulder and asked if I would please pray for her. I turned around and said, "Could I please do this in the morning as I am exhausted and need to get some rest? Tomorrow you can be the first one I pray for." She was quite insistent and began to tell me about her back and neck pain. I reluctantly placed my hand on her shoulder, mumbled some sort of a prayer, turned around and walked out the door. The next morning when I arrived at the meeting place she came running up to me to tell me the terrible pain she had endured for over a year was completely gone! Obviously in spite of my feelings God used me to heal this girl.

2. "Second, it is not a kind of gifting or personality type. We may regard certain people around us as persons of authority because they have an authoritative manner about them. The Christian's authority truly is a gift, but it is given to everyone in God's family and is not related to personality. Our spiritual authority is rooted in our position as members of God's family. It is ours whether or not we feel it, whether or not we have a special gift or personality type. All Christians have the right to both pray and relate to enemy forces in Jesus' name."[3]

Jesus' Uniqueness is Seen

The uniqueness of Jesus is seen in the following ways:

1   His power came from the Holy Spirit (Luke 4:14-18). He was baptized, anointed and empowered by the Holy Spirit.

2   His authority came from His relationship with the Father; He knew His identity and commission as the Son, sent from the Father; and this gave Him boldness to exercise His authority. Luke 3:21-22 quotes the Father as saying, "you are my Son, whom I love; with you I am well pleased."

3   His submission to the Father brought recognition by others of His authority. John 5:19 says, "Jesus gave them this answer. I tell you the truth, the Son can do nothing by himself; he can do only what he sees his Father doing, because whatever the Father does the Son also does".

4   His teaching was seen as authoritative because He spoke only what He heard from the Father (John 5:19).

5. His authority over demons, death, sin, sickness and nature was a result of obedience to the Father. (Mark 1:22, Matthew 9:6, Luke 8:24)

6. His life, death and resurrection disarmed the spiritual powers (John 12:31). With his exaltation, Jesus received from God all authority in heaven and on earth. (Matthew 28:18).

Jesus Restores Authority to Man

When Jesus ousted Satan, He restored man to his rightful position by bringing him into a new relationship with God and by delegating to him His own authority. In Christ the following things were provided to mankind:

1. We have new identity (sons/daughters - 1 John 3:1; Romans 8:16-17).

2. We have new position (seated with Christ - Ephesians 2:4-6).

3. We have a commission to go in Jesus' authority (Matthew 28:18, Mark 16:15-21, John 20:21):

    •   To proclaim the good news

    •   To baptize and teach

    •   To drive out demons

    •   To heal the sick

    •   To speak in new tongues

    •   To raise the dead

    •   To be Jesus to this world

4. Jesus has given us authority over the power of the enemy and nothing will harm us (Luke 10:19).

5. Like Jesus, we have power which comes from the gift and anointing of the Spirit (Acts 1:8) and we have authority which comes from our relationship with the Father through the Son (commission). Matthew 10: 1, 7,8

Release of Authority

There are certain principles that release us to exercise this God-given authority. When we neglect these principles the result is that there is a lack of authority.

1. Relationship with God is key: Consistently experiencing a growing and intimate relationship with the Lord must be an end in itself. It is impossible to operate in the power and authority of God if you don't know what God is doing and saying, and you can't know what God is doing and saying if you are not talking with Him and listening to Him. This is not something you do sporadically but must be done as consistently as you would to foster any intimate relationship.

   For instance, if your goal is to become an Olympic swimmer then you must not only spend significant time in the water swimming but you must spend significant time with the coach. The familiarity of your relationship is such that you often know what he wants you to do without having to speak. Likewise, you must learn how to spend time with God, waiting in silence and solitude. This will help you begin to understand that you are His Beloved and He wants to spend time with you. As the relationship grows you will see an increase in the release of authority and power in your life.

2. Faith in God's written Word (John 1:12): You must know and believe what God says about you in terms of your new identity, position and commission, and know and believe what God has done through Jesus in destroying the enemy and his works. Just believing God brings a release of authority.

3. Obedience to His Spirit: Obeying means doing what God says in the scriptures. It means listening for and obeying promptly the voice of the Spirit within you at all times. It means taking risks! Each time I do a model for healing prayer it is a risk. When I bring someone up to pray for them I rarely know what is going to happen.

   In the early stages of learning how to pray for healing I said to the Lord that I would pray as He led me. One Sunday morning during the invitation time for people to come for prayer a young man came forward and asked me to pray for his throat which was almost swollen shut. Before I began to pray God said to me, "I want you to put your hand on his throat and command it to be opened." I had never done anything like this so I said, "No way!" Again God repeated the same thing to me and with some degree of fear I did as He asked and commanded the throat to be opened. As soon as I said the words the throat was completely healed! Both I and the man I was praying for were ecstatic! This whole thing would not have happened if I had not taken the risk!

4. We must have an attitude of submission much like the Centurion in Matthew 8:9. The Centurion understood position, submission and authority. This means being under God's authority, being in harmony with fellow believers, receiving and learning from ministries God has brought into your life. This may even be ministries who have a style or approach with which you disagree.

5. A servant's heart (Matthew 20:25-28): Authority is released through service, i.e., what you do, not what you are. The question here in regards to the healing ministry is, "What is your

motivation?" Is it so you will look good or is it to minister the healing power of God to individuals and give Him all the glory?

6. Faithful service (Matthew 25:14-30): As you are diligent and persistent in what God has gifted and commissioned you with, you will find yourself moving into areas where there is a constantly greater operation of authority.

Although we have authority, we don't totally have the mind of God. God reserves the right to be sovereign. That's part of the reason not all of our prayers are answered, and why all are not healed when we pray. Even when we pray in great faith. We can care a great deal and we should, but we must remember that God is sovereign and He is responsible for what does and does not happen.

Furthermore, it is important that we not be presumptuous as we think of our authority. Jesus did not presume. For instance, don't tell people to stop taking their medicine. Rather you could suggest a visit to the doctor to determine whether the medication is still required. Do not claim things unless they are revealed as God's plan and confirmation is given. At the same time don't let fear of making mistakes or looking foolish keep you from taking risks.

One example of risk taking I remember very clearly in regards to "looking foolish" happened at a conference I attended in Anaheim, CA. A man I met there during the week was a carpenter and he had an injury to his eye caused by a splinter which the doctors could not remove. I prayed for him during the conference with no visible results. Late Friday night when the conference was over some friends and I were walking across the parking lot to our motel. My experience has been that when the Lord speaks to me He puts thoughts into my mind to which I respond. So the thought came that seemed to be Him speaking, "I want you to pray for Tom's eye." I said, "I don't want to pray for Tom's eye. I am tired and want to go home and go to sleep. Anyway, how am I going to find Tom? There are hundreds of us leaving at the same time and there is no way I can find him in this crowd." Guess what God said? "Stop and turn around!" I did, and Tom was walking right towards me! When he came up to me I stopped him and asked him if I could pray for his eye one more time. He agreed, but before I started the Lord conveyed to me that he wanted me to spit on my thumb and place it on Tom's eye and then pray for his healing. I was really hesitant to do this but I told Tom what I was going to do, all the while thinking how stupid I was going to look if God did not heal Tom's eye. I spit on my thumb, placed it on his eye and prayed with all the faith and fervor I could muster. After I removed my hand I asked Tom how his eye was and he said nothing had changed. I prayed again, with no visible change and then ended the prayer and headed back to the motel. On the way back I asked God, "Why did you do that to me?" He said, "Michael, you told me you would do anything I asked!" So, God had asked me to do something which I felt would make me look foolish to test me, so I would know if I would really obey Him.

The point of this example is that you will have to take risks if you are going to step out in obedience to what you sense God is asking you to do. What we do may not always look as if we have succeeded but the important point is that we learn obedience and we learn to take risks and as we take these risks we learn from them. In addition, God is honored by our obedience.

Remember:

You have the Authority and Power available to you! Learn how to use it!

Section 3: Physical Healing

Introduction to Physical Healing

To pray for Physical Healing requires that we take risks. It is scary to step out in faith, take the authority of Jesus and pray for the healing of someone standing there before you. Although Jesus commands us to heal the sick, we often respond by saying, "That's not my gift." If that is your response, you're right. But, it is a gift the Holy Spirit gives to us, and it is given as we step out in faith to exercise that gift. He increases its use and manifestation in us. There are many approaches to take in praying for healing. This section will hopefully provide you with some helpful tools to use in a healing prayer ministry.

Approaching Physical Healing

There are a diversity of ways in which people perceive, understand and approach healing. Therefore:

1. We need to be sensitive to the understanding and beliefs of those for whom we are praying.

2. We must become familiar with the scriptural examples of this diversity:

   * Luke 7:2-10: The Centurion knew Jesus had the authority to heal, even by His spoken word.
   * Luke 8:43-48: The woman subject to bleeding knew she only needed to touch the garment of Jesus to be healed.
   * Mark 1:40-42: The cleansed leper asked if Jesus was willing to heal him.
   * Mark 2:2-12: The man with palsy was let down through the roof and healed.

Yielded Vessels

God is the healer and we are the vessels used to accomplish His purpose.

1. Jesus demonstrated His power and authority over every disease and infirmity during His earthly ministry. (John 5:1-9, 9:1-7)

2. Jesus empowered and commanded His disciples to preach the Kingdom of God and to heal the sick. (Luke 9:1-2; Mark 16:15-18)

3. He who believes in Jesus will do the works that Jesus did, and greater works, asking in His name. (John 14:12-14)

4. The book of Acts records the ministry of the believers in the early church who were empowered by the Holy Spirit to heal the sick, cast out demons, and even raise the dead. (Acts 3:1-8, 5:12-16, 8:4-7)

5. The Great Commission of the Church to preach the Kingdom of God and to demonstrate the power of God in healing continues today. (Matthew 28:18-19, Luke 4:18-19)

Types of Prayers for Physical Healing

1. Prayer of Petition (Matthew. 7:7-11).

2. Prayer of Command (Mark 7:31-35, Luke 13:10-17, when a special anointing of spiritual gifting is operating).

    At one of our training workshops there was an individual suffering with severe migraine headaches. At one point during my teaching he was standing in the back of the room holding his head. The Lord stopped me in mid-sentence, I looked back at this man and said, "Spirit of Infirmity I command you to stop it and leave now!" Immediately the pain was gone!

This particular way of praying is a rare occurrence but when it is clear that God wants to heal this way it requires obedience on our part to His prompting.

3. Prayer of Deliverance (Mark 1:23-27). Jesus drove the evil spirit out of a man who was in the synagogue.

4. Prayer for inner healing whereby roots of bitterness or unforgiveness may have caused physical disease.

Other Elements Relating to Physical Healing

1. Often, when we are praying with people, we will place our hands on them in accordance with the following scriptures.

    Then one of the synagogue rulers named Jairus, came there. Seeing Jesus, he fell at his feet and pleaded earnestly with him, "My little daughter is dying. Please come and put your hands on her so that she will be healed and live." Mark 5:22-23

    His father was sick in bed, suffering from fever and dysentery. Paul went in to see him and, after prayer, placed his hands on him and healed him. Acts 28:8

2. Another biblical practice that we follow is to anoint with oil.

    They drove out many demons and anointed many sick people with oil and healed them. Mark 6:13

    Is anyone of you sick? He should call the elders of the church to pray over him and anoint him with oil in the name of the Lord. James 5:14

See page L-1 for more information on these topics.

The Power of The Testimony

There's a passage in Revelation 19 that says, "The testimony of Jesus is the spirit of prophecy." Revelation comes to give us consciousness of something before understanding of something. Prophecy by nature causes things. It's a catalyst to change or transformation. The verbal or written record of anything that God has done contains the spirit or anointing of prophecy. Keep in mind that prophecy causes. The testimony of Jesus carries with it the anointing to cause that testimony to be duplicated. A testimony carries with it an anointing for prophecy. It creates the potential for the miracle to be duplicated.

Psalm 78 When you give a testimony it releases the power of God to heal anything, not just those things having to do with that specific testimony. Remember that a testimony reveals the nature of God and His covenant with man. It's not just a story of power it's an invitation for an encounter. We have thought of testimonies as just a nice story not realizing the deep well that God was trying to dig in us about the power in the testimony.

Psalm 78:9…The children of Israel didn't keep the covenant of God, they refused to walk in His law. Why? They forgot His works. The courage for radical obedience comes from the consciousness of a miracle working God. A part of Israel's history was to talk about what God did and had done. Their conversation was to daily include stories about God. The works of the Lord were to be studied and engaged in until they become real to them. They become their story. Israel's job was to not lose consciousness of a God for whom nothing was impossible.

In this Psalm He was saying, "You walk with and serve a God who is with you in you and upon you and nothing is outside of His reach." And somehow if they could keep the commandment of the Lord in their conversation and they could keep the record of His invasions into human impossibilities, if they could keep that a part of their conversation everyday it would help them to never lose consciousness of the God who does miracles. And if Israel could keep that consciousness, that awareness, that realization cultivated continually in their life then they would not lose the courage for great risk and radical obedience.

Because Israel didn't remember the works of the Lord they lost the courage to walk in radical obedience. Nehemiah 9. "And they refused to obey, they were not mindful of your wonders." They could not live on the edge of radical obedience because they lost sight of the miracles and the wonders. The things for which we have no explanation. The things that cause us to go wow! Every time Israel fell into great immorality most likely we would find that at the root they stopped talking about the miracle working activities of God.

If we stop talking about the miracle working power of God we will expect it less. If we expect it less it will happen even less. If it happens even less we will talk about it even less. If we talk about it even less it will happen even less. There's this downward spiral that's guaranteed in every one of us personally, in our families and in our church life. You cannot live a day without an awareness of a God who does the impossible. We have been given an impossible task and only God has a right to expect fruit from a fig tree out of season. Without that awareness permeating all our values, all our thought processes, all our decisions we cannot do what God has called us to do. Everything that we are doing has to be inundated with that awareness. Only God has the right to expect impossible fruit. He's required of us things we cannot do on our own. Furthermore, we have the responsibility of bringing people into an awareness of those things that none of us can accomplish on our own.

Romans 8: 38 "For I am convinced that neither death nor life, neither angels nor demons, neither the present nor the future, nor any power, neither height nor depth, nor anything else in all creation, will be able to separate us from the love of God that is in Christ Jesus our Lord." Notice the intentional omission of things in the past. If you're going to live from the past you're going to have a deceptive experience that says, "God no longer loves you." Those who live under the influence of the past live under the influence of a lie. Paul says in ICor.3:21, "For all things are yours whether Paul or Apollos or Cephas or the world or life or death or the present or the future-all are yours, and you are of Christ, and Christ is of God." Why isn't the past mentioned. Because the past you have no legal right to. Any area of our life that does not have hope is under the influence of a lie. Hope is the joyful expectation of good.

One of the greatest tragedies I see in the church is people working hard and praying hard for what they already have. Never realizing the benefit of truly being born again, of being forgiven of sin. Psalm 119:11 "The testimony of the Lord is your inheritance forever." We have legal right to visit anything in the past, whether it's your past my past or Moses' past. We have legal access to all of it when it's been touched redemptively by God.

How many of you know that difficulties from your past that have been healed are now a testimony of grace. It is legal to visit as a testimony of grace but it's not legal to visit as a present problem because it denies the effectiveness of the blood of Jesus. Many, in wanting a move of God, revisit things of the past in order to feel humble and then come confessing things that are no longer on God's record books. They believe that to be a posture of humility that will bring a move of the spirit. How can I get a move of the spirit by denying the effectiveness of the blood of Jesus?

There's only one part of the past that you have legal access to and that's the testimony of the Lord. Anything that He has done in your life or anybody's life you have legal right to as a testimony. When you embrace those testimonies they become a part of you and it releases life. You've been impacted by an invasion of God in an impossible situation. By filling your heart and mind with the attributes of God's works that He has done, that thing becomes yours and as you share it, it's not merely the reporting of a story, it's imparting a revelation of the nature of God and the nature of His covenant with man. Every testimony contains those two things. Every testimony is an unveiling of the nature of God and a revealing of His covenant with man.

There is a third thing. From the midst of the revelation and covenant there's an invitation by God,"Come and know me in this way." Psalm 66:5 "Come and see the works of God..." He is sending out an invitation to see something that happened several years earlier. Right there is where we are going to rejoice. Let the stories in the bible become your story. Psalm 119:111 "The testimony of the Lord is your inheritance forever." It's your story.

Earlier I made reference to Revelation 19:10, "…The testimony of Jesus is the spirit of prophecy. The testimony carries with it the power to duplicate itself. In the Old Testament the word for testimony means, "do it again." The nature of testimony back in the Old Testament was do it again. Contained in the story is the power to do it again. In Revelation there is a passage that says "They overcame him by the blood of the Lamb and the word of their testimony." The blood of the lamb is the legal basis for all victory. This means that God's entire activity among men throughout history is my testimony. The record of God's invasion throughout all of history is my testimony. Learning how to pick up a testimony from history and through your own encounter with the Lord, your own prayerful meditation over that event, it becomes your story and that becomes part of your arsenal that sets you up for victory for cities and nations. This is one of the tools He has given us.

We do not realize that we are sitting with a loaded cannon. We've been using a pea-shooter not realizing what we have in our arsenal. The stories that are given are revelations of God. What kind of revelation do you want hanging over your city? These stories are a prophecy that contain a revelation of God's nature and you must create a culture that values these stories. If that value is not placed on it, you will not draw the people to you with the stories. You must embrace the value of those stories yourself. Miracles will turn cities around and testimonies create the room for it.[1]

Does Everyone Get Healed?

1. Jesus healed all who came to Him (Matthew 4:24, 8:16; Mark 1:32; Luke 6:18-19).

2. There were special times when the power to heal was present, even by Peter's shadow or Paul's handkerchief (Acts 19 11-12; Acts 5:15-16).

3. Jesus healed only one man at the pool of Bethesda when there were many present who were sick. His response for the one being healed was that He only did what the Father was doing (John 5:1-20).

4. Jesus heard His Father's voice perfectly. We are still in the process of learning to hear His voice and to follow Him. The important point for us is to be open and sensitive to what the Father is doing (John 5:19).

Hindrances to Healing

I heard Francis MacNutt say, "The greatest mystery about healing is that we don't know what we are doing." There are many things about the healing ministry that we do not understand. We do not understand why some are healed and why some are not healed. We have discovered that there are some things which can hinder healing. I don't want to imply that these can be used as an excuse when someone is not healed but may help to explain why the healing is not taking place.

1. Lack of Faith (Matthew 17:14-20)- Jesus upbraided His disciples when they couldn't heal the epileptic demoniac because of their lack of faith.

2. Unconfessed sin can restrict God's desire to heal, James 5:16: "Confess your sins to one another and pray for one another that you may be healed".

3. Asking amiss or not praying specifically , James. 4:3: "When you ask you do not receive, because you ask with wrong motives, that you may spend what you get on your pleasures."

   - We may not know the root problem of the sickness.
   - We may not be praying in God's timing.
   - We may be praying for physical healing when a spirit of infirmity is present.

4. Transgressing the Natural Laws of Healing —— Perhaps we abuse our bodies with poor eating habits, lack of exercise, anxiety and worry that continue to cause physical problems.

Various Manifestations of Healing Through Prayer

1. Healing that comes through spiritual or emotional healing due to the close relationship between our bodies and our emotional and spiritual health

2. Healing that comes through the speeding up of the natural healing forces at work in the body

3. The gradual healing of a severe ailment that would ordinarily require surgery or other means to heal

4. Immediate healing by a creative miracle of God or gift of healing

Remember: Our responsibility as Prayer Ministry Team Members is to be obedient to the Holy Spirit as we believe God is leading us to pray and to leave the responsibility of any results to God.

Steps in Ministering Healing

The process we have learned to follow in ministry is essentially a combination of prayer ministry outlined by John Wimber in his book <u>Power Healing</u>, adaptations from Dr. Francis MacNutt's model, and experience that we have gathered along the way as we have been ministering to people in our particular church setting. The following general guidelines will help to outline this process.

First Step

The First step is the interview. Obviously, the easiest way to determine what to pray for is to simply ask the recipient, "What would you like us to pray for?" or "When did this condition start?" This is an important time, so don't rush it in your attempt to begin praying. This time not only provides important information, but gives the prayer recipient a little time to feel comfortable. As we listen to the recipient, we begin to get some understanding of the problem. As we are listening we are also asking God specifically how He wants us to pray for this person. We do need to be careful not to spend too much time in the interview, especially if there is a limited amount of time available to pray.

Second Step

Next we invite the Holy Spirit to come and help show us how to pray. We are asking Him to be in charge. Though the prayer recipients have expressed what they desire prayer for, often there are additional things God will reveal to us as we pray. When you audibly invite the Holy Spirit to come in the presence of the prayer recipient, this helps them to understand that it is God who is doing the work.

After inviting the Holy Spirit to come, we do not immediately jump in and start praying; instead WE WAIT for His leading. It is not unusual to feel the power and presence of the Spirit. Sometimes this is reflected in the prayer recipient by a slight trembling of their body. Sometimes this is felt by those praying. The slight trembling of hands may be witnessed or there may be sensations of "heat" in the hands. In some cases the recipient may even feel weak or need to sit down or will "rest in the Spirit." None of this is unusual but quite common manifestations of the presence of the Holy Spirit.

During this time of waiting we begin to get some understanding of the problem. Please realize that we will only obtain a partial understanding of what's going on. As the prayer continues we will often receive greater insight with regard to praying more specifically or praying for something which the prayer recipient has not even mentioned.

Third Step

The next step is to pray as the Holy Spirit leads you. We will begin to determine how to pray. It may simply be to begin with the person's request or God may have revealed another place to start. If the person is fearful you may need to begin by praying for them to relax, for Jesus to give them peace.

During this time we have found it best to pray with our eyes open. This allows us to observe any visible signs in the prayer recipient that God is working and helps guide us in our praying.

If the prayer recipients are comfortable we can lay hands on them. If you are not sure they are comfortable with this, simply ask them. This is especially recommended in the case of praying for physical healing. The practice is usually to lay hands on the place where it hurts. If it is not appropriate to lay hands over the area of the physical body of the one for whom you are praying, you can ask the recipients to lay their hands there and place your hand over theirs. There is nothing magical about this, but we have found that it communicates love and often acts as a direct channel of God's healing power. It is not unusual for the prayer recipients to feel tingling or heat in the place where the injury is located.

As you are praying there is nothing wrong with stopping to ask if they are experiencing any sensations at all. It is all right to interrupt the prayer to ask questions. It does not stop the flow of God's power. By asking, we can determine whether or not God is indeed doing something. This will help us to know if we are praying in the right direction and if we should continue or begin to wrap it up. When you have finished all that you know to pray then stop.

Fourth Step

The Blessing. We find this step to be of immense value in ministering to the prayer recipient. Sometimes we simply say, "I bless you in the name of the Father, the Son, and the Holy Spirit", or "In the Name of Jesus, I bless you with His peace, love and forgiveness." This may be uncomfortable for you; but we believe, through Christ, we have this authority. Often during prayer we will ask God to bless them with a deeper experience of His presence, with a fullness of His Spirit. It is not unusual to see them visibly relax and a sense of peace or joy come over them. Some are healed at this moment.

Fifth Step

Post-Ministry Follow-up. We need to give direction for several things. First of all, for problems that may occur after the ministry session. The prayer recipients need to know that they can take authority in case symptoms return. This is especially important where there has been some deep inner healing. This type of healing is often a process over time and they need to know how to deal with the memories, emotions, attitudes or habits that will attempt to return and bring back the hurt.

We need to affirm those who are not healed. They especially need to be encouraged and loved. We always ask them to come back for further ministry. We never communicate that the lack of healing is because they didn't have enough faith, or that there is "sin in your life." Though sometimes this can be the case, God will reveal that to them in His timing.

Follow-up is especially important for those who have gone through deliverance ministry. Unless they can remain strong and persist in prayer, in God's Word and in their authority in Christ, the demons will usually return. See page 6-15 for more information on how the liberated can remain free.

One of the most important lessons we are learning is to follow up with those we have prayed for with a phone call, a note, or a visit. Obviously this isn't always feasible, but should be done whenever possible. We consistently encourage people to return for prayer, whether there has been no visible improvement or some small improvement.

How To Operate in the Word of Knowledge

Discerning the Voice of God.

Often when we approach this topic people will respond with, "I don't hear from the Lord," or "I don't know how to discern what He is showing me from the other thoughts that are coming into my mind." We are much more discerning than we realize. You may be receiving Words of Knowledge long before you understand what they are. When you are first learning how to pray for people you may discover that as you pray a word or picture will come into your mind. When you begin to share these revelations with the person you are praying for they will often respond in a way that confirms that what you just spoke to them was correct.

"At one point a friend explained to me that as I prayed for people what I was receiving from God were Words of Knowledge. The Lord was teaching me how to hear his voice. When I first started paying atten-

tion to these promptings of the Holy Spirit I would receive a single word. Soon came sentences and sometimes pictures. I have discovered through trial and error that as I pray with people and step out and speak those words that come into my mind, that most of the time it is the Lord speaking."

If the Lord is giving you specific discernment or clarity on a particular item as you are praying with someone then you need to take the risk and speak what you believe you are receiving from Him. This can be done in such a way that the person you are praying for can confirm it or not. They may respond with, "That was right on, how did you know that?" or "That doesn't mean anything to me." Be aware that sometimes what you have just spoken to them may be something they do not remember from their past or something that they do not want to deal with yet. In either case you simply go back to prayer.

When I am praying with someone I often say: "I believe the Lord is giving me this word, or picture, or name, etc., does this mean anything to you?" This is especially helpful when you are learning to discern the Lord's voice from your own. What is important is that you take the risk and begin to speak.

As you take the risk and speak those words you are receiving you become more adept at discerning what is from God and what is not. Also, as you spend more time with God you will learn to discern His voice from others because of your relationship with Him. Relationship is key to hearing from God. The more time you spend with Him the easier it is to discern His voice.

For example, I can be in a room full of people that are all talking at once. If my wife is talking close enough for me to hear her I can pick her voice out from the others even if I cannot see her. That is because we spend significant time together and have an intimate relationship.

We can mistakenly get the impression from scripture that God only speaks to men and women of biblical stature and importance in the Kingdom of God. The reality is that God wants to have as intimate and communicative a relationship with you and me as He does with His son Jesus

How Do I Know That is God?

When we pray and begin to learn how to listen we can have three voices going through our head: our own, God's and Satan's. Therefore, we must learn to discern which is which. It is important to understand that God's voice will be positive, affirming, encouraging and unrushed. Satan's voice will be negative, condemning, discouraging and may call for impulsive or hurried behavior. Our own voice is often those things that we already know about the person we are praying for but refuse to believe because we are familiar with what the person is dealing with. The ability to discern is given to us by the Holy Spirit when we become believers. As with many of the gifts it develops with use.

Often when we are ministering with people, God will give us insight into a particular problem or area of ministry that he wants to deal with. There are things that we hide from the world but God knows the heart and sometimes reveals those hurts to us for the purpose of ministering to that need.

We need to be cautious as to how we approach these things that God is showing us. Sometimes this insight may be for the purpose of intercession until an opportune time and sometimes we are to minister to the need at that moment. This is where keen discernment comes into play. We need to listen carefully to what God is telling us and determine what to do with it.

I was ministering at a retreat and participants lined up for prayer. As I walked down the line and prayed for people, the Lord would give me specific things to pray for. It was not unusual for people to come to me afterward and ask how I knew that particular thing was an issue in their life. In some cases, as I prayed He would reveal something about them that He just wanted me to know but not necessarily pray for at that moment. Often these were things, which needed to be prayed for in private because of their sensitive nature.

The Lord Is Always Speaking

The Lord is more determined and excited to speak to us than we are to hear from Him. We must realize that God is always speaking, but He is not human and His first language is not English! If we can grasp this revelation and realize that most of us don't really know how well we can see and hear God, we can begin to "tune our receivers to His station."

For example, in the room you are in right now there is music playing all around you. But even if you were to close your eyes and listen very carefully, you would not be able to hear it. However, by simply turning on a radio, you would be able to hear what was there all the time. The reason, of course, is that our human bodies were never designed to hear radio waves. Having the proper equipment allows us to tap into a realm that exists with us even though we can't hear it with our naked ear. In the same way, God is always speaking to us! We have the ability to hear what He has been speaking to us all along but were unable to perceive before.

Have you ever been in a situation where you are talking with somebody and you get this overwhelming feeling that you need to pray for them? Sometimes it is no more than a fleeting thought or a feeling. God speaks to us in different ways and we need to be expecting Him to give us discernment into situations on a daily basis.

Maybe it's that feeling you get when you know that something isn't right or you know something before it happens. Maybe you walk in a room and your heart jumps or you get an uneasy feeling. In many instances this is spiritual discernment. God is showing you that something is not right. We need to recognize when these things happen and take some action. For example, occasionally I will meet someone and although in the physical realm we may greet each other and talk amicably, inside my spirit is telling me to be cautious around this person. I pay attention to these feelings and react accordingly, perhaps limiting what I share or ending the meeting quickly.

How The Gifts Grow In Your Life

The gifts of the Holy Spirit are not awards! You cannot earn them. Because the gifts are not a mark of maturity, you do not have to wait for your life to be in perfect order to receive them. You are instructed however to passionately pursue them.

There is a principle that Jesus laid out in the parable of the talents, which is this; if you use what you have received, more will be given to you. If you do not use what you have, even what you have will be taken away from you.(Mt. 25:14-28) This principle applies to every aspect of the kingdom of God. If you want to receive a deeper level of revelation, then you must be faithful with the level of insight that you have now! There are some who have only received one talent who spend all of the time trying to figure out why someone else got more then they did instead of working with what they have been given to attain more!

You cannot grow in the gifts of the Spirit without making mistakes! We gain experience as we step out in faith when we are learning to listen to the Holy Spirit.

In my own life I have gained much wisdom by the mistakes I have made on the road I have traveled. God uses our life experiences to give us wisdom and intends for us to use that wisdom to minister to others. "I am a somewhat impulsive person by nature. Because of this I've gotten myself into difficult or embarrassing situations. Over the years I've learned how to control this impulsive behavior. I've not changed from being impulsive; I've just learned when to go with the impulse and when to wait. Now that's wisdom."

There is a story of a banker who had reached the age of retirement and was about to be replaced by a young man. Upon his arrival to take the helm from his predecessor, he asked the older man how he became successful. The man replied, "Good decisions." "How do you make good decisions?" the young man asked. "Experience", he replied. The young man thought for a moment and then inquired, "How do you get experience?" With a warm smile, aged with wisdom he replied "Bad decisions."

Suggestions for Practicing

You can practice words of knowledge for healing in a group setting by simply praying and asking the Lord to show you anyone who is experiencing illness or pain. This can come as a simple word, sentence, or picture. It can come as a sensation in your body that directly coincides with the part of someone else's body that the Lord wants to heal. If it is appropriate in the meeting, ask the group if anyone has that specific problem. If so, you are then able to pray for that person and see what the Lord does.

Kris Vallotton in his book, "A Call To War!"[2] suggests that you go to a restaurant or public place of business and pray for the person who is waiting on you. Ask the Lord for words of knowledge for the person. It is usually best if you do this when the person is not in your presence. Write down the words of knowledge on a piece of paper. Later, when they return you can ask them questions concerning the words of knowledge you received. For example, if you felt like the Lord showed you that the person has 3 children, you can simply ask them if they have children. If their answer is yes, you can inquire how many, etc. When you are first learning, I would suggest you not tell the person that you have words of knowledge from God! In the beginning, this practice is more about you growing in your gift then it is about ministering to the person you are talking to. As your ability to hear the voice of the Holy Sprit improves, you will begin to step out in boldness and faith.

When we teach on hearing from the Lord we often break down into groups of three and ask the Lord to reveal something about one of the people in our group. Typically, over 90% of the people hear something that is confirmed by someone in their group. Sometimes it will be a word that seems rather ridiculous and has no deep spiritual meaning.

Once while practicing this with a group I went around the room and questioned each individual regarding what they had heard. One young man said, "I saw a glass table shattered all over a patio. I thought that was really ridiculous until I shared this with my group. One of the people in my group responded that her glass patio table had broken just before she left for this meeting!"

When you think about it this is not something that has deep spiritual meaning. There was no particular need for prayer of a physical or emotional pain. But the point is that he was willing to be obedient and say what he saw even though it seemed to him to be ridiculous. Again, as you are willing to step out and risk you will see this gift increase.

On other occasions we are given words or pictures that go right to the root of the problem. One participant in a training session wrote:

We split up into groups of three strangers and then asked the Holy Spirit to give us a word for someone in our group. I struggled with trying to clear my mind and really be receptive to the Holy Spirit. After a while of listening the word 'suitcase' came into my mind. I told it to the other guys and one of the members in our group said that when he was leaving for the trip packing his suitcase was a great source of consternation for him and his wife. There were various other examples in the room that seemed more powerful and relevant. The most striking was a woman who received the word "Teddy Bear" before Mike even split us up into groups. Then, in a room of 300 people, the Holy Spirit led her to a man whose daughter had called him Teddy Bear when she was young. There appeared to be a strained relationship there that the Spirit was speaking directly to.

If you are willing to step out and begin to speak what you believe you are hearing you will be amazed at the number of times your "words" are right on target. The more you take the risk and speak what you are hearing the more you will grow in this gift. Remember that relationship is key to hearing from God. The closer your relationship, the easier it is to discern when He is speaking to you.

Section 4: Repentance

Repentance Is Vital

Why is repentance so vital for those who minister with prayer teams? The answer is that un-repentance gives Satan a place where he can and will operate in our lives.

> *And the angels who did not keep their positions of authority but abandoned their own home - these he has kept in darkness, bound with everlasting chains for judgment on the great day. Jude 6*

> *For if God did not spare angels when they sinned, but sent them to hell, putting them into gloomy dungeons to be held for judgment, . . . 2 Peter 2:4*

When Satan rebelled against God, he was placed under eternal judgment in "bonds of darkness." The devil and his fallen angels have been relegated to moral darkness, because they are eternally separated from God, who is LIGHT.

This darkness to which Satan has been banished is NOT limited to areas outside of humanity. When we accepted Jesus as our Lord and Savior, Colossians 1:13 tells us, "He has rescued us from the dominion of darkness and brought us into the kingdom of the Son He loves."

When we harbor sin, the light in us is then in darkness. *"Satan has a legal access, given to him by God, to dwell in the domain of darkness. . .* The devil can traffic in any area of darkness, even the darkness that still exists in a Christian's heart.[1] *God will bring things into our lives to change these dark things, but we have to open the door, by faith, and let Him in to work.*

Demons are always standing by to "help" the Christian persist in their sin, to destroy all of the fruits of the Spirit, and thus enlarge the darkness. They are constantly vigilant, looking for an opening to gain greater influence in a person's life. We, as prayer ministers and intercessors, need to deal with all areas of darkness in our own lives before we intercede on behalf of others; the areas we hide in darkness are the areas of our future defeat. We must be discerning of our own hearts and walk humbly with God, particularly when we have been called to prayer ministry and intercession. The Holy Spirit is a gentleman and He will not intrude to bring change; He comes in only when invited.

Humility and Submission

> *But He gives us more grace. That is why Scripture says, 'God opposes the proud, but gives grace to the humble.' Submit yourselves, then, to God. Resist the devil, and he will flee from you. Come near to God and he will come near to you. Wash your hands, you sinners, and purify your hearts, you double-minded. James 4:6-8*

The greatest defense weapon we can have against the devil is an honest heart before God. A clean heart is essential for an unobstructed relationship with the Lord. Sin breaks the relationship. When the Holy Spirit shows us an area that needs repentance, we must overcome the defense instinct. We must silence the personal defense lawyer within us who pleads, "My client is not so bad, in fact only human." If we listen to this we will never see what is wrong and never face what needs to change in our lives. Our self-preservation instinct has to be surrendered to the Lord because Christ is our only true advocate. If we allow the Holy Spirit to bring conviction, rather than arguing with Him, our heart becomes more pliable before God. This requires that we humble ourselves and admit our wrongs. If we are too proud to humble ourselves then God is opposed to us (James 4:6).

One of the principles that is painful to new prayer ministers and intercessors is this: **God is not in a hurry**. He takes the time He needs to build His character in us, to patiently and methodically clean our hearts so that we can pray His purposes for others. As Cindy Jacobs says in <u>Possessing the Gates of the Enemy</u>, "Most of us want everything to happen immediately, but God loves to marinade. He wants tender hearts in His living sacrifices. The problem with living sacrifices is that they want to jump off the altar. They sit there awhile and begin to sniff; after a little longer they realize it sometimes hurts to be conformed to the image of Jesus."[2]

Look back at James 4:6-8. We often hear RESIST and FLEE as a testimony to spiritual warfare, but it is in the context of repentance, humility and a clean heart that we see Satan fleeing. We must model for those to whom we minister an attitude of humility and submission to God. As Francis Frangipane says in <u>The Three Battlegrounds</u>, "We must go beyond a vague submission to God; we must submit the exact area of our personal battle to Him."[3]

"When we come against the power of the devil in our lives, in the lives of others, in our homes, in our churches, in our schools and in our communities, we must come with a heart in complete submission to Jesus. To further quote Frangipane, "Victory begins with the name of Jesus on your lips; but it will not be consummated until the nature of Jesus is in your heart."[4]

Satan will continue to come against the area of weakness until we realize **God's only answer is to become Christlike**. As we appropriate the name and nature of Jesus, our enemy will withdraw. Satan will not continue to batter you if the circumstances he designed to destroy you are now working to perfect you.

As we minister in healing prayer, we need to constantly be praying the prayer of King David in Psalm 51:10 - 11. We also need to be prepared to teach those to whom we minister the importance of a clean heart.

> *Create in me a clean heart, O God, and renew a steadfast spirit within me. Do not cast me from your presence or take your Holy Spirit from me.*
> *Psalm 51:10-11*

Section 5: Inner Healing and Forgiveness

Introduction to Inner Healing

Often when we are praying for people we discover that there is a need for inner healing, that is healing in the emotional core. The Bible refers to our emotions as our heart. So put very simply, inner healing is healing in our heart.

> *For I am poor and needy, and my heart is wounded within me. Psalm 109:22*
>
> *The Lord is close to the brokenhearted and saves those who are crushed in spirit. Psalm 34:18*
>
> *He heals the brokenhearted and binds up their wounds. Psalm 147:3*

All of us who live on earth have been subject to some degree of pain in our lives. Certainly it is not measured out in equal doses. Some people cannot even recall a time in their lives when they were happy while others appear to have pretty smooth sailing most of the time. However, nobody gets by without any pain at all, and it is not unusual for hurtful incidents of the past to affect us physically, psychologically and spiritually in the present.

The repentance issues discussed in Section 4 of this manual have to do with the attitudes, actions and words that come out of our own heart which cause pain and wounding to other people. Inner healing deals with our response to what has been done to us.

Here are two definitions of inner healing:

From John Wimber: "While sickness of the spirit is caused by what we do, sickness of the emotions is generally caused by what is done to us. It grows out of the hurts which are done to us by another person or some experience we have been exposed to in the past. These hurts affect us in the present, in the form of bad memories, and weak or wounded emotions. This in turn leads us into various forms of sin, depression, a sense of worthlessness and inferiority, unreasoning fears and anxieties, psychosomatic illness, etc. Included in this are the present-day effects of the sins of the parents in the blood line of a person. Thus healing of past hurts touches the emotions, the memories, and the person's blood line."[1]

From Francis MacNutt: "The basic idea of inner healing is simply this: Jesus, who is the same yesterday, today and forever, can take the memories of our past and

1. heal them from the wounds that still remain and affect our present lives;

2. fill with His love all those places in us that have so long been empty, once they have been healed and drained of the poison of past hurts and resentment."[2]

It needs to be made clear that it is possible to deal with some issues of emotional pain strictly between an individual and the Lord. But there are many people who have no idea why they feel the way they do. They cannot recall the roots of their pain, not to say anything about facing the issues and dealing with them.

Inner healing is a truth encounter with God. He is the Wonderful Counselor (Isaiah 9:6) who was there when we were knit together in our mother's womb as we are told in Psalm 139:13. Psalm 139 also declares in verse one, "Oh Lord, you have searched me and you know me." And in 1 John 3:20b we read, "For God is greater than our hearts, and He knows everything."

In praying for inner healing we are not trying to change the past. Our past is our past. We are asking God to change our response to the past and to heal the pain. We can also according to Romans 8:28 release our past into God's hands and ask Him to use it for good in the present and the future.

The Roots of Persistent Hurts

Some of life's hurts come simply from the fact that we live in a fallen world. Things happen such as accidents, disease, poverty and natural disasters that for the most part are not the result of someone's deliberate choice.

When I was ministering at a church in England a young man came forward for prayer. He shared that as the result of an auto accident the doctors told him he had a serious neck injury and if he moved his head there was a good possibility he would be paralyzed. This young man was traumatized by those words. He went home, did not leave his house, lost his job and was desperate to know what to do. We prayed and God gave us a very clear answer. I shared with him what God had shown me, then I prayed for a spirit of fear and trauma to leave him and instantly he was healed. He was able to freely move his head and neck around without any pain and the fear was gone!

Another major source of wounding comes from sins that are committed against us. Some actions and words are deliberately meant to hurt us. People say things like, "you're a loser, you cannot do anything right." There may be verbal, physical or sexual abuse that deeply wounds us. There are times people have no idea that they are causing us pain by what they do or say.

Lastly, there are those results of our own wrong choices and responses. Perhaps we have been involved in drugs, pornography or the Occult. When we participate in these activities we open ourselves up to emotional wounding and demonic spirits which can harass and influence us to further evil.

Some of these hurts go far back into the past; others are quite recent or even current. Many of the deepest hurts go back to times when we were most vulnerable and least able to defend ourselves. The most obvious of these times is childhood, but others include times of illness, pregnancy, trauma or when we are going through some kind of crisis.

SATAN DOES NOT PLAY FAIR! He thinks nothing of striking again when we are down. The old saying that when it rains it pours is often indeed the case.

It also appears to be true that it is those people who are highly significant in our lives that have the potential to cause the deepest wounds. For many the root source of emotional pain stems from their relationship to one or both parents. But for others it is some other important person such as a grandparent or baby-sitter, an educator, a sibling, a friend, a spouse, a child, a boss or co-worker, a pastor or church body.

Charles Kraft in his book <u>Defeating Dark Angels</u> talks about the common way most of us deal with these hurts and what would be the ideal solution. The following is a paraphrase of his words.

"As we go through life, we get hurt. When this happens, we do our best to keep from falling apart or behaving in a socially unacceptable way. Our honest reaction often gets suppressed, so that we can cope, but this becomes counterproductive later.

"This process is similar to bandaging a wound without first cleaning it. The wound festers and becomes infected under the bandage and then it leaks, allowing the infection into our current life. Ideally, we would deal honestly with each hurt soon after it happens by facing our true feelings, admitting them to God, and allowing Jesus to take charge and clean the wounds. In Matthew 11:28 he invites us to come to Him with all of our heavy loads and in Matthew 6:14-15 he makes it plain that we are to forgive anyone who has hurt us. Unfortunately we do not ordinarily do this and we leave hurts to fester so that we see disruptions later."[3]

Inner Healing in the Church-Is it Necessary?

What do we see in the Church that supports the need for inner healing?

We have in our congregations people who have truly been converted, who have walked in the presence and the power of the Holy Spirit, who read their Bible and pray, yet who have persistent problems such as a haunting sense of worthlessness, or who live in a state of anxiousness or fear, or who struggle with compulsive behaviors, etc.

There are many Christians for whom it is very difficult or impossible to reach out and minister to others. There are numerous Christians whose lives show very little or no visible fruit.

The emotional baggage that many people carry effects their relationship with God, their feelings about themselves, and their interactions with other people.

It is difficult to tell someone else that God loves them when you don't feel lovable or loved yourself. How do you encourage someone else that victory is possible in their life when you are walking in defeat? How do you share with someone that "Jesus is the answer" when that doesn't seem to be the case in your own life?

How Inner Healing Fits into the Christian Walk

The subject of inner healing stirs up a certain amount of controversy in the Body of Christ because many believe that when you are born again you are a new creature in Christ (2 Corinthians 5:17), that Christ's death on the cross took care of everything - and it is finished! It **is** true that Christ's work in providing our salvation was finished through His death and resurrection and that when we accept Him as our Savior our salvation is secured for eternity. But is that moment of asking Him into our life all that there is to the Christian walk?

Dr. J. Sidlow Baxter has said that our salvation has three tenses.

> *Therefore, since we have been justified through faith, (past) we have peace with God through our Lord Jesus Christ, through whom we have gained access by faith into this grace in which we now stand. (present) And we rejoice in the hope of the glory of God. (future) Romans 5:1-2 (parenthetical words added)*

Dr. Baxter made the following statement in a talk that he gave at Bakersfield Christian Life Center:

1. Past: "There is one sense in which salvation is instantaneous (justification). At the very moment we accept Christ, our sins are pardoned, our guilt is washed away and we are justified through the merits of Calvary's sinless Sinbearer."

> *But because of his great love for us, God, who is rich in mercy, made us alive with Christ even when we were dead in transgressions - it is by grace you have been saved. Ephesians 2:4*

> *But when the kindness and love of God our Savior appeared, he saved us, not because of righteous things we have done, but because of his mercy. He saved us through the washing of rebirth and renewal by the Holy Spirit, whom he poured out on us generously through Jesus Christ our Savior, so that having been justified by his grace, we might become heirs having the hope of eternal life. Titus 3:4-7*

Quoting Dr. Baxter again:

2. Future: "Finally at the return of Christ salvation in its consummative aspect (glorification) is to give sinless hearts, perfected powers, immortal bodies, and `faultlessness' before the Majesty on high."

> *Listen, I tell you a mystery: We will not all sleep, but we will all be changed - in a flash, in the twinkling of an eye, at the last trumpet. For the trumpet will sound, the dead will be raised imperishable, and we will be changed.1 Corinthians. 15:51 - 52*

> *Dear friends, now we are children of God, and what we will be has not yet been made known. But we know that when he appears, we shall be like him, for we shall see him as he is. 1 John 3:2*

> *He will wipe every tear from their eyes. There will be no more death or mourning or crying or pain, for the old order of things has passed away. Rev. 21:4*

But what about the here and now? Dr. Baxter says,

3. Present: "In another sense salvation is progressive (sanctification): for when we receive the Savior the Holy Spirit implants a new spiritual life and nature within us, and there is to be growth in spiritual power, understanding, usefulness and Christlikeness."[4]

When we accept Christ our spiritual status has changed. We have come out of the kingdom of darkness and death and now are a part of the Kingdom of God, a kingdom of light and life. However our mind, will, emotions and body were not instantly perfected. We are meant to experience a continuing work of Christ in these areas.

> *And we, who with unveiled faces all reflect the Lord's glory, are being transformed into his likeness with ever-increasing glory, which comes from the Lord, who is the Spirit. 2 Corinthians. 3:18*

> *Instead, speaking the truth in love, we will in all things grow up into him who is the Head, that is, Christ. Ephesians 4:15*

> *Do not conform any longer to the pattern of this world, but be transformed by the renewing of your mind. Romans 12:2*

> *. . . we take captive every thought to make it obedient to Christ. 2 Corinthians. 10:5*

> *. . . being confident of this, that he who began a good work in you will carry it on to completion until the day of Christ Jesus. Phil. 1:6*

Jesus Himself explains it in Matthew 13:33:

> *The kingdom of heaven is like yeast that a woman took and mixed into a large amount of flour until it worked all through the dough. Matthew 13:33*

Salvation is like yeast; once it enters our life it is meant to be worked through until it permeates all of our being.

Dealing with inner healing issues is part of the sanctification process that is going on in our lives as Christians. The following passage from Ephesians 4 is what inner healing is all about.

> *You were taught, with regard to your former way of life, to put off your old self, which is being corrupted by its deceitful desires; to be made new in the attitude of your minds; and to put on the new self, created to be like God in true righteousness and holiness. Therefore each of you must put off falsehood and speak truthfully to his neighbor, for we are all members of one body. In your anger do not sin: Do not let the sun go down while you are still angry, and do not give the devil a foothold.*

He who has been stealing must steal no longer, but must work, doing something useful with his own hands, that he may have something to share with those in need.

Do not let any unwholesome talk come out of your mouths, but only what is helpful for building others up according to their needs, that it may benefit those who listen. And do not grieve the Holy Spirit of God, with whom you were sealed for the day of redemption. Get rid of all bitterness, rage and anger, brawling and slander, along with every form of malice. Be kind and compassionate to one another, forgiving each other, just as in Christ God forgave you. Ephesians 4:22-32

Biblical Examples of Inner Healing

It is easy to overlook the inner healing that takes place in the Bible, but it is there. It requires us to stop and consider those whose lives Jesus touched. What was happening to them emotionally when they encountered Him? Most of them would never be the same again.

First of all let's consider in general all those who were physically healed by Jesus. Many of them had lived with their illness, paralysis, blindness etc. for years. What did it mean to them to be singled out and healed by Jesus? How did that effect how they saw themselves? What were the emotions they were dealing with daily before their healing? What emotions welled up inside when they realized their ordeal was over?

Consider the leper in Mark 1:40-42. He had a contagious disease that isolated him from the mainstream of society. He was appalling to look at. Surely he wrestled with loneliness, rejection and fear, perhaps he was bitter at his lot in life, we know for sure that he had little to look forward to and then he learns of Jesus.

A man with leprosy came to him and begged him on his knees, "If you are willing, you can make me clean." Filled with compassion, Jesus reached out his hand and touched the man. "I am willing," he said. "Be clean!" Immediately the leprosy left him and he was cured. Mark 1:40-42

When Jesus, filled with compassion, touched the man, did the most significant healing happen to his body or in his heart? I think the most significant healing was emotional.

Consider the woman caught in the act of committing adultery and taken to Jesus (John 8:1 - 11). She was being used by the Pharisees to bait Jesus. Surely she knew her behavior violated the Law of Moses and just as surely she knew that the penalty of adultery was death. What was she feeling standing there before Jesus? Afraid? Degraded? Guilty? Ashamed? Probably she was experiencing all of these and more. After Jesus dealt with her accusers and they left, He turned His attention to her.

"Woman, where are they? Has no one condemned you?"
"No one, sir," she said.
"Then neither do I condemn you," Jesus declared. "Go now and leave your life of sin." John 8:10b-11

Suddenly, she was free, she was clean, she could start over again, there was hope and highly likely, there was peace.

Once, when I was ministering at a maximum security prison in California I had just finished the message, given the invitation for people to receive Jesus into their lives and was finishing up praying with someone. This rather small, timid man slowly made his way up to me, reached out his hand and tugged on my shoulder. As I turned around he said, "Can I ask you a question?" I nodded. He said, "When I asked Jesus to forgive me of my sins did He forgive all of them?" I said, "Yes." He replied, "You mean all of them?" I said, "Yes." He said, "Wow, all of them!" As he turned away from me and walked back down the aisle I heard him saying over and over, "Wow, all of them." He could not comprehend that Jesus had forgiven all of his sins.

Consider Matthew who took advantage of his fellow Jews for his own personal gain. Used to being an object of hatred, what did it mean to him, when Jesus said in Matthew. 9:9, "Come, follow me." In the eyes of most he was a worthless traitor, but when Jesus looked at him, he saw a disciple and the future writer of one of the gospels.

Consider Zacheus, another tax collector. The people in his town openly called him a sinner. It is significant that the Bible points out that he was short. In Zacheus' eyes this was a physical deficit. In the narrative in Luke 19:1-10 it is necessary for him to climb a tree in order to get a glimpse of Jesus. But it is the very fact he is in the tree that attracts the attention of Jesus who says, "I must stay at your house today." Suddenly, here is someone who accepts him as he is and wants to have fellowship with him. He is transformed. Jesus says, "Today salvation has come to this house, because this man, too, is a son of Abraham. For the Son of Man came to seek and to save what was lost."

Consider Mary Magdalene. There is no Biblical record of her actual encounter with Jesus. We are simply told in Mark 16:10 that she was the one "out of whom he had driven seven demons." It doesn't take much imagination nor is it stretching probability to surmise that if Mary had seven demons inside her when she met Jesus, she was a bit of a mess. It is also highly likely that she did not see herself as having a great deal of value.

What the Bible does tell us is what she was like after Jesus freed her. She was able to care about others and to be a part of a group. In Luke 8:2 we are told she was part of a group of women who traveled with Jesus and His disciples. She was also able to give, helping to provide financial support for Jesus' ministry. She was standing near Jesus' mother when He was crucified (John 19:10). She watched Joseph of Arimathea prepare Jesus' body for burial (Matthew. 27:61). She was among the first to arrive at the empty tomb. She was told by an angel that Jesus had risen from the dead and then sent to tell his disciples (Matthew. 28:1 - 8). And Mark 16:9 and Matthew. 28:9 tell us that she was the first person Jesus appeared to after the resurrection. She had gone from a life of inner turmoil to being honored to be the first to know the good news that Jesus was alive!

Finally, consider Peter. Consider Peter because unlike all the above examples where healing occurred when the person had their initial encounter with Jesus, Peter was already a believer (Matthew 16:16 "You are the Christ, the Son of the living God."), and he was highly committed to Jesus (Matthew.

26:35 "Even if I have to die with you, I will never disown you.") when disaster struck. As Jesus had predicted (Matthew. 26:34), he denied three different times that he even knew Jesus. And when that reality hit Peter as the rooster crowed, the Bible tells us that he went out and wept bitterly (Matthew. 26:75). A believer who has failed! How many of us can relate to Peter? It would be a bitter story indeed if it ended there, but it doesn't.

In John, chapter 21, we find the disciples back on the Sea of Galilee fishing just as they were when they first met Jesus. And this time He meets them there again. He has built a fire and prepared breakfast for them on the beach. And in what should be an incredibly significant moment for all of us, Jesus takes the initiative to reconcile their relationship. It isn't really made clear until verse 20, but Jesus and Peter have come apart from the group and are walking along the beach. This was a time of Jesus making it clear to Peter that he was forgiven, and still loved and valued by the Lord. In declaring his love for Jesus, Peter is restored as a committed believer and best of all, Jesus isn't finished with him yet. He still has plans and purposes for Peter's life. He has a new role for him. When he commissioned him before, it was as a fisher of men, but now he is to be one of the shepherds over the flock, the church in Jerusalem.

Jack Hayford points out in his book <u>The Power and the Blessing</u> that there was a reason why Peter's failure didn't destroy him. The answer is in Luke 22:31. Before predicting that Peter would deny Him Jesus says this, "Simon. Simon, Satan has asked to sift you as wheat. But I have prayed for you, Simon, that your faith may not fail. And when you have turned back, strengthen your brothers."[5]

Jesus not only predicted Peter's denial but also his victory, "when you have turned back." And what was it Peter had going for him? Jesus was praying for him!

Two scriptures which should cause every believer to shout for joy tell us that we have the same thing going for us!

> *Who is he that condemns? Christ Jesus, who died - more than that, who was raised to life - is at the right hand of God and is also interceding for us. Romans 8:34*

> *Therefore he is able to save completely those who come to God through him, because he always lives to intercede for them. Hebrews 7:25*

Who is this Savior, Jesus, who is interceding for us? Does he understand the pain, the hurts, the wounds that we experience? This is how the prophet Isaiah portrays Him.

> *He had no beauty or majesty to attract us to him,*
> *nothing in his appearance that we should desire him.*
> *He was despised and rejected by men,*
> *a man of sorrows and familiar with suffering.*
> *Like one from whom men hide their faces*
> *he was despised and we esteemed him not.*
> *Surely he took up our infirmities*

and carried our sorrows,
yet we considered him stricken by God,
smitten by him, and afflicted.
But he was pierced for our transgressions,
he was crushed for our iniquities;
the punishment that brought us peace was upon him,
and by his wounds we are healed.
We all, like sheep, have gone astray,
each of us has turned to his own way;
and the Lord has laid on him the iniquities of us all. Isaiah 53:2-6

Forgiveness - The Key to Inner Healing

Therefore, the kingdom of heaven is like a king who wanted to settle accounts with his servants.
As he began the settlement, a man who owed him ten thousand talents was brought to him.
Since he was not able to pay, the master ordered that he and his wife and his children and all
that he had be sold to repay the debt.
The servant fell on his knees before him. 'Be patient with me,' he begged, 'and I will pay back ev-
erything.' The servant's master took pity on him, canceled the debt and let him go.
But when that servant went out, he found one of his fellow servants who owed him a hundred
denarii. He grabbed him and began to choke him. 'Pay back what you owe me!' he demanded.
His fellow servant fell to his knees and begged him, 'Be patient with me, and I will pay you back.'
But he refused. Instead, he went off and had the man thrown into prison until he could pay the
debt. When the other servants saw what had happened, they were greatly distressed and went
and told their master everything that had happened.
Then the master called the servant in. 'You wicked servant,' he said, 'I canceled all that debt of
yours because you begged me to. Shouldn't you have had mercy on your fellow servant just as I had
on you?' In anger his master turned him over to the jailers until he should pay back all he owed.
This is how my heavenly Father will treat each of you unless you forgive your brother from your
heart. Matthew 18:23-35

From the Lord's Prayer:

Forgive us our debts, as we also have forgiven our debtors. Matthew 6:12

This is the only portion of the prayer that Jesus comments on afterwards (Matthew 6:14-15). "For if you forgive men when they sin against you, your heavenly Father will also forgive you. But if you do not forgive men their sins, your Father will not forgive your sins."

The teachings of Jesus were extraordinary because they were often the opposite of what we naturally think is right. The following quote from the Sermon on the Mount was meant to have a revolutionary effect in our hearts and minds.

You have heard that it was said, 'Love your neighbor and hate your enemy.' But I tell you: Love your enemies and pray for those who persecute you, that you may be sons of your Father in heaven. Matthew 5:43-45a

We Are Forgiven

In him (Christ) we have redemption through his blood, the forgiveness of sins, in accordance with the riches of God's grace that he lavished on us with all wisdom and understanding. Ephesians 1:7-8

Therefore there is now no condemnation for those who are in Christ Jesus, Romans 8:1

For he has rescued us from the dominion of darkness and brought us into the kingdom of the Son he loves, in whom we have redemption, the forgiveness of sins. Colossians 1:13-14

We Are to Forgive

Bear with each other and forgive whatever grievances you may have against one another. Forgive as the Lord forgave you. Colossians 3:13

Be kind and compassionate to one another, forgiving each other, just as in Christ God forgave you. Ephesians 4:32

Most of the ground Satan gains in the lives of Christians is due to unforgiveness. We are warned in Ephesians 4:26-27, "In your anger do not sin: Do not let the sun go down while you are still angry, and do not give the devil a foothold." In the parable from Matthew 18 quoted above, the unforgiving servant is handed over to the jailers or as the King James translation says "to the tormentors." In the same way when we refuse to forgive we find ourselves in bondage to and being tormented by such things as guilt, striving, fear and bitterness.

To Forgive or Not to Forgive

To forgive those who have caused us great pain is not an easy thing. It goes against our sense of justice. It is not fair. They deserve to be punished. However, Jesus is asking us to forgive others because of His grace and mercy in forgiving us. We deserved to be punished and it wasn't fair to Him that He had to go to the cross on our account, but He was willing to do that (John 10:17-18).

There are some important things to know about forgiveness

First of all, to forgive doesn't necessarily mean that we are going to forget. Our past is our past. But it does mean that we are not going to hold the offense against that person any longer. We are going to release it and let it go!

A number of years ago I was deeply wounded by a friend. He did not even know that what he said and did caused me hurt and pain. I internalized my feelings and excused his behavior by saying such things as, "That's just the way he is, so get over it." I found that I began to feel a wall going up in my relationship with him. Although in my time of prayer I had forgiven him, when I thought about the event all those hurt feelings would surface. About three years after this happened I was on vacation with my wife. Early one morning I was sitting out on the deck having coffee and listening to some music. Suddenly his favorite song came on and I felt as if I had been punched in the stomach. I started sobbing and all those feelings came to the surface. I knew I had to release them, forgive him and let God heal the hurt. The next time I saw him, though I remembered the event, those hurt, angry feelings were not there and I felt as if the wall had been broken down.

Forgiving is not pretending that the offense didn't matter. Part of genuine forgiveness is to face the hurt and to realize that even after you forgive you may have to continue to live with the consequences of that offense.

Forgiving does not necessarily mean the person is entirely off the hook. You are releasing them from your anger into God's hands. God, who is much wiser and far more capable of handling things then we are, is left in charge.

Forgiveness is a choice. It is a crisis of the will. It is also a crisis of trust and obedience. It is our Lord, our Master, it is Jesus who is commanding us to forgive. Would He command us to do something we were incapable of doing? Do we trust Him to have our best interest at heart as He gives us this command?

The truth is that forgiving benefits both the forgiver and the forgiven. Gary Smalley and John Trent have written, "As long as people are angry at each other, they are chained to each other." [6] They are talking about being emotionally chained. We literally drag them around with us emotionally and the act of forgiving sets both them and us free. Note that at the end of the parable of the unforgiving servant both servants end up in jail.

A pastor recently referred to carrying bitterness as "emotional suicide." Job 18:4 says, "You who tear yourself to pieces in your anger. . ." The fact that anger harms the person who is angry is not just a Biblical truth but a widely accepted psychological and medical fact. In her syndicated column Ann Landers printed this little gem of truth, "Anger is like acid. It does more harm to the object in which it is stored than to the object on which it is poured."

The truth is that the person you are angry with may not even be aware of your anger. They may have no idea and suffer no ill effects of your anger at all, while it eats away at you daily.

> *Do not judge, and you will not be judged. Do not condemn, and you will not be condemned. Forgive, and you will be forgiven. Luke 6:37*

Even though you understand that your own personal emotional healing depends on your willingness to forgive, it may still be a very difficult thing for you to do. But if you are willing and ask the Holy Spirit to help you, He will help you get to the point where you can forgive.

Jesus is our example.

> *(On the cross) Jesus said, "Father, forgive them, for they do not know what they are doing." Luke 23:34*

> *When they hurled their insults at him, he did not retaliate; when he suffered, he made no threats. Instead, he entrusted himself to him who judges justly. 1 Peter 2:23*

Steps to Forgiveness

The following steps are helpful both in your own personal walk and as you minister with others.

1. *Make the decision that you want to forgive and be set free.*

2. *Pray and ask the Holy Spirit to bring to mind people and events, etc. that He knows are the roots of the anger in your heart.*

   It is highly likely, especially if there are a lot of issues there, that everything will not be revealed at once but over a period of time.

   Deal with who or what He shows you. Be on the alert when things you haven't thought about in years suddenly come to mind. If something that comes is painful, allow the pain. If you feel like weeping, then do so.

3. *Identify specifically what it is you need to forgive a person for and what was the response on your part to that offense. This is a crucial step.* Don't just say, " I forgive you, dad," but "I forgive you dad for not being there when I needed you. I felt so rejected and that I was not very important to you at all." Being specific helps us to identify the wound which helps as we pray for healing.

   We may have to forgive the same person for many different things. Or we may on different occasions have to forgive the same offense, especially if the same offense is continuing to occur.

   Then Peter came to Jesus and asked, "Lord, how many times shall I forgive my brother when he sins against me? Up to seven times?"
   Jesus answered, "I tell you, not seven times, but seventy times seven."
   Matthew 18:21 - 22

We will never be done forgiving. It is part of the Christian lifestyle.

4. *Be honest before God in regards to how you feel about the person or the event.* God knows it all anyway. Nothing is going to surprise him and you need to get it out and lay it before him.

   David Seamands says, "There is nothing you can share out of the agonizing hurts and depths and hates and rages of your soul that God has not heard. There is nothing you can take to Him that He will not understand. He will receive you with love and grace."[7]

   Trust in him at all times, O people; pour out your hearts to him, for God is our refuge. Psalm 62:8

   Nothing in all creation is hidden from God's sight. Everything is uncovered and laid bare before the eyes of him to whom we must give account.
   Hebrews 4:13

5. *Forgive the offense.* Get alone in a place where no one can hear you and out loud talk to the person you need to forgive just as if they were in the room with you. Tell them that you forgive them and what it is you are forgiving them for. If the person has died you can still forgive them. You are still alive and forgiving them frees you from the burden of unforgiveness. Obviously, we cannot repent and ask a person to forgive us after they are gone, but you can ask God to forgive you.

    Praying out loud will help you in the future to remember that as an act of your will, you did forgive the person.

6. *Pray and ask God to forgive you for holding the unforgiveness in your heart.* He will forgive you.

    If we confess our sins, he is faithful and just to forgive us our sins and cleanse us from all unrighteousness. 1 John 1:9

7. *Forgive yourself.* One of the most difficult things for people to do is to forgive themselves for their part in their pain.

    Maybe you realize you have some guilt in regards to what you have forgiven another person for. Maybe you made a choice at some point in your life and you have been living with the consequences ever since. Maybe you have made your own life a lot more difficult than it needed to be. Maybe you have caused another pain and it grieves you to the core of your being.

    Jesus died on the cross in order that your sins could be forgiven. You must forgive yourself, because if you don't, you are in effect rejecting His gift. You are refusing to appropriate and walk in the forgiveness He has provided.

8. *Deal with your anger towards God Himself.* It is necessary to face this issue which Christians find very difficult indeed. What are those things you are holding against God Himself?

    Neil Anderson teaches that, "Technically, we don't forgive God because He cannot commit any sin of commission or omission. But you need to specifically renounce false expectations and thoughts about God and agree to release any anger you have toward Him."[8]

    It is hard for us to admit that we hold things against God, but we do. We blame Him for how things have gone. We wonder where He was when certain things happened. Why didn't He prevent them? Sometimes we are angry about how He made us, or the parents He gave us, or we believed He would do something and He let us down.

    You need to identify the issues you have with God. You need to ask His forgiveness for your anger towards Him. You need to accept that forgiveness.

9. *Pray for healing.* Forgiving is like lancing a boil. It allows all the infection and pus to come out and then you treat it with medicine to bring healing. Once you have forgiven someone,

it is time to pray and ask Jesus to heal the wound. Loose His Holy Spirit to fill the voids in your life, to bring comfort, to fill you with the love and the realities of the acceptance and forgiveness of Jesus. The healing process may take some time, but welcome and rejoice in it.

10. *Begin to pray for the person you have forgiven.* If they don't know the Lord, pray that they will come to know Him. Pray for blessings for them. Pray that Jesus will help you see them through His eyes.

A Word of Caution

We need to be very careful about approaching the person we have forgiven. It is one thing to go to someone to repent and ask their forgiveness for something you've done, and quite another to confront someone with the fact you are forgiving them. If the person is unaware of how you feel, it is best to deal with it between you and the Lord and leave it there.

If it is someone from whom you have been estranged and you would like to reconcile, pray extensively about it first. This is an extreme example but it is meant to illustrate a point. It doesn't aid in reconciliation to approach someone and say for example, "I forgive you for being an insensitive jerk."

A much better approach is to confess that you've been angry and have asked God's forgiveness and would like to ask theirs. Let them know that they mean a lot to you and you would like to reconcile. They may or may not forgive you or apologize to you. Be prepared for that and let it go.

As we are set free from the pain in our own life, we don't want to inflict pain on someone else in the process.

Forgiveness is part of the Christian walk. It is a wonderful provision for us that allows us to be free in the mercy and grace of Jesus.

Some Practical Helps When Praying For Inner Healing

It is important when we pray for healing in a person's heart and mind that we remember that it is God the Father who among His many attributes is all-knowing; it is Jesus Christ who is called the Wonderful Counselor, the Great Physician, the way, the truth and the life; it is the Holy Spirit who Jesus told us is our Teacher, our Comforter, and our Helper. IT IS GOD WHO HEALS. We are His vessels, His servants, and His friends. We are simply coming through prayer with the person we are praying for into God's throne room to lift that person and their needs before the Lord. This is not dependent on our ability to be a great counselor.

A Model For Praying for Inner Healing

In this section we will present a model for praying for emotional healing when it is highly likely this will be a one time experience. Often this occurs when you pray for people who respond to an altar call, or someone expresses a need for prayer in a class or some other setting, or a friend simply says, "Will you pray for me?"

1. Begin with a short interview. What is their need or request? How long has this been going on? Were they going through any kind of crisis when it started, etc. Ask them how they would like you to specifically pray.

2. In prayer ask the Holy Spirit to come and be in charge of this prayer time.

3. Wait on the Lord. Spend some time in silence listening for how He would lead you to pray.

4. If He gives you a specific way to pray then be obedient to that leading, if not then begin to pray over the specific request that caused the person to ask for prayer.

5. Stop and ask the person if God is telling them anything or bringing specific people or events to mind. If there is a need to forgive someone, or repent of an action or attitude on their own part, then encourage them to do this. Pray for God to heal any woundedness. If they have repented, pray that they will experience in a very freeing way Christ's love, acceptance and forgiveness. If God brings to mind any specific scriptures that apply to their situation share those with them.

    If He has given you a specific word for the person share it by prefacing it with "Does this make any sense to you?" Even if the person says, "No, it doesn't" don't assume you've heard wrong, God may in time reveal to them what it means.

6. Return to prayer and pray over any specifics God has revealed. Even in those times when we feel we haven't a clue as to how God wants to work in their specific situation, there are many things that we know from God's word are His will for all of us. Pray for His continuing work and blessing for their life.

7. Encourage and bless the person. Encourage them that God does indeed want to move in their life, encourage them to continue in their walk with the Lord, and if you feel led to, encourage them to seek further prayer or specific help.

When Once Is Not Enough - On-going Ministry

Just as in the case of physical healing, sometimes healing in the emotions can come miraculously and instantly and sometimes it comes over a period of time. The concept of soaking prayer or on-going prayer is helpful here too.

Sometimes when you are involved in a prayer ministry you notice that the same person is coming for prayer over and over and over again. Sometimes it is for the same need, sometimes it is for one thing after another. Then there are times when you pray for someone and you realize, "This is just the tip of the iceberg." For example, you sense that while you've prayed over one thing there is within this person deep-seated bitterness, or perhaps fear, or their self worth was so low it was difficult for them even to receive prayer, etc. Sometimes someone will ask if you will pray for someone that they know has many and sometimes desperate needs in their life. This section is about times like these when a ten to fifteen minute prayer time is not enough.

Wholeness Ministries is always quick to note that the way we have come to do things is not the only way to do it. In this section we will share our model for on-going prayer ministry while at the same time encouraging you to seek the Lord on how you are to proceed.

When it has been established that an individual needs <u>and wants</u> on-going prayer they are assigned to a prayer team. We put together a team of two or three of our trained prayer team people after they have individually prayed about being on this particular team and agree to make the commitment. There are advantages in having the same team pray for the person each time. Trust is built, the person only needs to share their story once, and confidentiality, which is of the utmost importance, is easier to maintain. Once we have a team we make an appointment for the person to come for prayer. While occasionally we make an exception, most appointments last between an hour and an hour and a half. If someone is coming from out of town, for example, we might set aside a morning or an afternoon.

We recommend beginning with no more than a six or eight week commitment. Sometimes even that is not necessary. In the privacy of the appointment God sometimes accomplishes very quickly what needs to be done. As the initial commitment nears its end a decision can be made whether or not to continue. If the person is experiencing healing, if issues are being dealt with, if they are cooperating in the work God is doing in their life and you feel He isn't finished yet, then continue a while longer.

If little has happened in your times together or if you are unsure whether or not you should continue, then take a break for an indefinite period of time. Express a willingness to pray with the person again in the future and put the ball in their court to call you when they would like to continue.

It is difficult when you realize that someone is really enjoying and being encouraged by the prayer sessions, but no real progress is being made towards healing. It is very easy to get locked into an on-going ministry that has no apparent end in sight. There are also times when it seems the demonic actually sends someone our way who literally drains the time and energy of many people. Be on guard against this type of thing. It is not the purpose of the ministry to have people become dependent on the team members, nor to have team members locked into never-ending commitments. In cases like these bring the sessions to a close. If there is someone or someplace else that you know of where the person might find help then suggest that they try there. Bless them, then release them to Jesus.

When You Pray

One of the most crucial things to instill in prayer team members is that prayer ministry must be done in the love of Jesus. Charles Kraft says, "For if what we do isn't loving, it isn't being done in Jesus' way. . . . Jesus used His power to show His love."[9]

The other crucial thing is that what is said and done during the prayer times must be kept confidential between the individual and the team. Nothing will destroy a prayer ministry faster than a breach of this trust. If there are any legal issues involved—for example, there are laws in the state of California which require certain people such as nurses and educators to report child abuse—these should be called to the person's attention before ministry begins.

If you have set up your ministry so that a pastor or board or Task Force oversees it and prayer team members can go to them for help, then explain this up front to the person you are praying for. Or if you find yourself unsure of how to handle a certain situation, ask the individual if it's all right if you discuss this with - and then name the specific person. The advantage of praying as a team is that you have each other and can together intercede on behalf of the person you are praying for. However there should be a plan in place as to what happens when a prayer team feels like they are in a situation that is over their heads.

It is helpful to have a notepad and pen handy during these sessions. You may want to make note of some details of their story, or things you want to come back to later. Sometimes the Lord will give you a word and you will want to jot it down so you won't forget. Occasionally prayer team members use notes to pass information to each other rather than talk with each other and interrupt the flow of the ministry that's taking place.

Three Cautions

Some of the things people share in ministry sessions that have happened to them or that they have been involved in can be quite appalling. It is really important to keep your cool. People tend to shut down very quickly and no longer be open to ministry if they think you are shocked and can't handle what they are telling you.

Do not condemn the person even if it is very obvious that sin has played a major role in their problems. Remember how Jesus dealt with the woman caught in the act of adultery in the book of John, chapter eight, verses one to eleven. Minister to the person with love and compassion and in due time the Lord will bring the right moment to lead them to repent and receive His forgiveness. Focus on God's willingness to restore their relationship with Himself.

Don't believe everything everyone tells you. For various reasons people do not always tell the truth when answering the questionnaire (see page G-1 for a copy of the Questionnaire) or the questions asked during prayer sessions. In many cases they simply do not trust you enough when ministry begins. It is not unusual after you have spent some time together that they will tell you they did not tell the truth or that they left information out. If you suspect someone is not being totally honest, pray about it during your own private prayer times with the Lord. Ask Him to bring out the truth during the ministry sessions. If you know the person is not being honest, lovingly confront them.

The Prayer Team Session

The Opening Prayer

The first moments of a prayer ministry session are of course ones of greeting and light conversation to help the person get comfortable, but you will want to move into a time of prayer very early on. It is important to ask the Holy Spirit to be in charge of your time together. Express the collective desire of everyone there that the individual you are praying for be brought into freedom and wholeness, able to be the person God created them to be. Pray for protection for everyone involved in the session and their families. Pray that God's Kingdom will come and His will be done in your time together. Allow for moments of silence. Often each member of the team will pray, sometimes the person who has come for prayer will pray also. This is wonderful when it happens because it helps to focus the person on the Lord, to express their own desire for Him to work in their life, and helps prepare their heart to receive from Him.

If the individual appears apprehensive, then address that in your prayer and ask Jesus to bless them with His peace.

Pray - Interview - Pray

The session will go back and forth between times of interviewing and times of prayer. We are asking the Lord to do a work in the person's life; to set them free from the wounds of the past that are affecting them in the present, to set them free from those sins and habits that have them enslaved, to perhaps free them from demonic oppression (see the section on deliverance), and to bring His light and truth, love and healing into every area of their lives. We are asking Him to reveal the roots of their pain so that they can forgive, repent of, or renounce whatever it is that has them bound up. Then we want to lead them to accept and receive all that Jesus has for them.

This process of seeking the roots of their pain involves asking lots of questions. It involves learning to listen two ways, to listen carefully to what the person is telling us and at the same time listening carefully to what the Lord is telling us. The most important thing is to remember that this is prayer ministry. The majority of the time should be spent praying not talking to each other. If we ask the Lord to reveal things, He often does, sometimes right while we are praying, sometimes later. It is not unusual to have a person come to the next week's session with something the Lord brought to mind during the time between sessions.

Wholeness Ministries has developed a Prayer Ministry Questionnaire (see page G-1) which we often use in this process. Sometimes we send it to the person we will be praying for and ask them to fill it out and return it to us before we meet. Sometimes we have them bring it to the first session. Sometimes we use it as an interview guide and our team will ask them the questions and fill in the answers as they talk. They also read and sign the Release Agreement. See page (H-1) for a copy of the Release Agreement.

Two Important Questions

It is very helpful to know where the person you are praying for is in their walk with the Lord. Simply ask them early on to share with you how they came to know the Lord. Their answer will tell you lots of things. If they are a believer ask them what their current walk with the Lord is like. If they are not sure that they have ever asked Jesus into their heart, ask them if they would like to be sure. Then lead them in praying to accept Christ. Encourage them to record the day they made this decision in the inside of their Bible. If they don't have a Bible make an effort to see that they receive one.

If it turns out they are not a Christian and are not ready to make that decision yet, go ahead and pray for and minister to them. This often leads to their making a decision shortly down the road.

The other important issue has to do with whether or not the person's will is engaged in the healing process. Do they want to be healed? Quite frankly, if they don't really want to be healed, if they are not willing to co-operate with the Lord in bringing about healing, not much is going to happen.

Ask them what they are expecting or hoping will happen in your time together.

It may be necessary from time to time to do a little bit of teaching. You might need to explain what repentance is or what forgiveness is and is not (see page 5-11) or what it means to renounce something (see page 6-13). Many believers have never read the Bible so don't assume they know everything it has to say.

Two Way Listening

The term two way listening means that we want to listen to both what the person is telling us and to what God is telling us. If it is the desire of our heart to learn to do this, God can help us become more proficient at it. If God is calling you to be an intercessor, a prayer team member or both, then pray for discernment - the ability to perceive or recognize clearly (Webster's New World Dictionary).

Listening to God

In its simplest definition prayer is conversing with God. It should involve both times of speaking and times of listening. The key is to learn to recognize God's voice.

Before we ever go into a prayer ministry session we should spend some time with the Lord. If He brings to our mind any things we need to repent of or anyone we need to forgive, then we need to take care of those things. We need to pray over the person we are going to be praying with, asking that the desires of Jesus' heart for that person be fulfilled.

When we begin the actual time with the person we always pray right from the start that God will lead and be in charge of our time together. Therefore we should not be surprised if we hear from Him. Often it is simply by a thought that He places in our mind, sometimes an impression on how to pray, sometimes a specific word that tells us what the problem is, sometimes a picture in our mind, sometimes a scripture that fits the moment perfectly.

Caution: When we feel God has told us something, we need to ask Him (in our minds, not out loud), "What do you want me to do with this?" Sometimes He will urge us to share it, sometimes it is Him revealing things to us and we are not to share it at that moment in time.

If you feel you are supposed to share what you have seen or heard, do so in a gentle way. Preface it with words like, "I think God is telling me . . .", "Does this make any sense to you . . .?", "Let me share this picture I just saw . . .", etc. If it is indeed from the Lord it will often be confirmed by someone else in the room. Or the person being prayed for will say that it is right on target. However, even if it is not confirmed, don't assume it wasn't from the Lord. Simply suggest something like, "Well, we will have to pray about that one" and go on with the session. It is not unusual for the meaning to become clear later on.

Sometimes, especially when we are just beginning to move in these areas of ministry, we mistake our own thoughts as coming from God, but if we are careful in how we share them it allows us to test them. When things we share are confirmed by others then it helps us learn what was indeed God's voice. As we walk with Him and listen to Him, His voice becomes more and more familiar and we become more confident that it is Him.

The man who enters by the gate is the shepherd of the sheep. The watchman opens the gate for him, and the sheep hear his voice. He calls his own sheep by name and leads them out. When he has brought out

all his own, he goes on ahead of them, and his sheep follow him because they know his voice.
John 10:2-4

Listening to the Person

The very first time we meet with someone for prayer, the big question is where do we begin? The most obvious answer is with whatever it was that motivated them to come for prayer in the first place. While we want the emphasis and the majority of the time to be spent in prayer, it is necessary to let the person tell their story. It is also helpful to go over the Prayer Ministry Questionnaire (see G-1) with them.

Just as we can learn to grow in our discernment of God's voice, we can become more adept at listening to people and hearing those things that may be the keys to their healing. This section will talk about some of the things that you can learn to tune into as people talk. Please do not be discouraged by its length or think that you have to memorize or know it all. As you learn about and become aware of these things, the Holy Spirit can call them to your attention during ministry times. Remember at all times we want Him to lead these sessions and not to be relying on our own intellect.

Two Cautions

- We do not need to know all the garbage and all the details of a person's life. If they start sharing things you don't need to know, then simply stop them and explain that it is not necessary to tell you all of that. Don't probe for details especially when it comes to sin in which they have been involved. It is sufficient to know that it was a part of their life and needs to be dealt with.

- Be careful not to take the burdens of the one you are praying for on yourself. It is essential to learn to pray for others, including interceding for them between sessions, without carrying them and their troubles on your own shoulders. You do this by releasing them to Jesus. He is our Lord and Master, He is in charge.

What Are We Listening For?

Please be aware that this is not an exhaustive list nor is it in any special order. These are simply common things you will hear that may be keys to unlock the chains that have the person bound.

- *Events*: Listen for key events in the person's life that brought about major changes. These might include such things as marriage, divorce, a death of someone they were close to, an accident or other trauma, a move, etc.

- *Relationships*: All of us have people who are very important in our lives. Take note if any key relationship in the person's life is very difficult or broken.

- *Unforgiveness*: It is highly likely that the person is holding something against one or more individuals. It will be necessary at some point to deal with these forgiveness issues. The person may well be holding things in their heart against God and against themself. These too will need to be dealt with in order for healing to come.

- *Destroyed Dreams - Disappointments*: If life has not gone the way the person expected or hoped, that is often the root of some unforgiveness and resentment.

- *A Neglected Relationship With God*: If a person is a Christian but not walking closely with the Lord it may simply mean they have allowed other things to have priority in their life, or it may mean that they are angry at Him or feel guilty or afraid.

- *Satan's Lies*: Listen for lies and deceptions that the person believes are true. These often are misconceptions of God, or beliefs that are contrary to what the Bible teaches, or lies about themselves. We often find people believe that they are worthless, that God can not possibly forgive them after what they've done, that their situation is hopeless.

  It is also very common for people to have wrong ideas about God. It is especially difficult if they have not had a good relationship with their earthly father to relate to God the Father. More than once people have expressed that they don't have any problem with Jesus but they are afraid of God the Father. There is no understanding of the Trinity and that Jesus shows us what the Father is like. Listen for these types of things.

- *Inner Vows:* An inner vow is a deliberate decision that sets the will in a certain direction. At some point in time a decision was made that usually includes the words "I will never" or "I will always". Some examples would be things like, "I will never allow myself to be hurt like that again", "I will never be like my mother", or "I will always see that my kids have everything that they need." Even if the basic intent of the vow seems good, these vows need to be renounced by the person and broken by the power of the Holy Spirit. They have a binding effect on a person's will that needs to be broken in order for the person to be free to become all that God meant them to be.

- *Sin:* Pray for discretion in confronting the person with their sins. When you feel it's the right time, do it gently and without condemnation. Remind them of God's provision for their sins, the death and resurrection of Jesus, and of God's willingness to forgive. Lead them into repentance and acceptance of God's forgiveness.

We need to be cautious because if we confront them too soon or too harshly it may shut down further ministry. On the other hand we can not ignore the role sin is playing in their life.

- *Personality Extremes:* If you notice that the person has a personality trait that really catches your attention and seems to be extreme, pray over why they are that way. Some examples would be a person being extremely shy or fearful, or you might notice that they always want to be in control or that they are a perfectionist. Maybe they always blame someone else for everything that happens to them. Other common traits are being arrogant, having a superiority or inferiority complex, someone who is overly dependent on someone else, someone who can't make a decision, or someone who is extremely individualistic. Pray that God will reveal the roots of these traits.

- *Emotions*: As people talk, listen for the emotions or feelings that they are expressing. Some of the most common are listed below.[10]

- *Abandonment*: From their point of view someone was not there when they needed them. They could even feel abandoned by God.

- *Rejection*: Even if the rejection is not expressed in words, it is perceived. Marriage partners feel rejected when divorced, parents feel rejected when a child rebels, a child or an employee may feel rejected when corrected all the time.

- *Inadequacy*: In the person's eyes they don't measure up to the expectations of others or even their own standards. Often the fact that they don't measure up has been directly communicated to them.

- *Guilt:* In some cases a person carries guilt because there is sin in their life. However a person can also feel guilty if they didn't live up to someone else's expectations, or they may feel like it's their fault that a trauma occurred (for example, a divorce). Some people feel guilty that they were even born, perhaps their birth created a hardship for their parents. Victims often feel that they were somehow the cause of the abuse they suffered.

- *Shame*: Something has happened in the person's life that has left them with a deep sense of dishonor or disgrace.

- *Anger, bitterness*: Anger has its roots in real or perceived mistreatment. It can be directed towards oneself, other people, at a set of circumstances or crisis, at life in general, or at God Himself.

- *Depression*: Depression has its roots in anger.

- *Fear*: Fear is usually a result of trauma or a response to having to deal with angry people.

- *Rebellion*: Rebellion can also be a response to dealing with angry people. The person has difficulty with authority figures. It can also be caused by abuse or neglect, by jealousy (often of a sibling), or by the legalistic pressure to conform.

- *Jealousy*: Often overlooked, this is a powerful emotion. The person perceives that they didn't get their fair share of something. It may be over material things but more commonly it is over things like love and attention.

- *The Desire To Escape*: The person feels life is so bad or unpredictable that they would rather escape. Often they escape through addictions or some type of pleasurable activity. Sometimes, if they perceive their situation as hopeless, they do consider suicide. Encourage them by sharing the truth of God's Word. Pray over them that God will break through their darkness with truth and hope and light.

Then you will know the truth, and the truth will set you free. John 8:32

- ***The Occult***: Take note of any involvement or reference to anything that has to deal with the occult or a non-Christian religion. The Prayer Ministry Questionnaire will bring many of these issues to light. Pay attention to any bizarre behavior or any changes in the sound of their voice or the look in their eyes. It is not unusual for a person carrying unresolved emotional issues to have something demonic oppressing them as well. It is important that you be very familiar with the material in the deliverance section (see page 6-1) of this manual when you are doing on-going prayer ministry.

Remember: IF SOMEONE NEEDS INNER HEALING THEY MAY OR MAY NOT NEED DELIVERANCE, BUT IF SOMEONE NEEDS DELIVERANCE THEY WILL ALWAYS NEED INNER HEALING.

Start Praying

Sometimes as you listen to a person's story the Holy Spirit makes it very clear as to what you need to begin to pray. Sometimes you are not sure. If He hasn't given you any special instructions then begin with the issue for which they asked prayer. Try to find out when the problem began. During a teaching time in Bakersfield, California Francis MacNutt shared that he often asks the person, "Have you always been unhappy?" This technique will get them reflecting on when things were going pretty well in their life and will help to identify when things changed.

Sometimes the person is very clear and knows exactly the root of their problem; they just haven't been able to deal with it. Help them be very specific about what happened and how it made them feel. Help them identify who all was involved that they are holding things against. Ask about their own role in what happened, because often times anger is directed inward and they need to forgive themselves. Try to help them recognize anything they are holding against God Himself.

As is needed and as you feel the Holy Spirit is leading you, lead them to pray forgiving all who need forgiving, repenting of anything they need to repent of, renouncing any thing they need to renounce. Then a prayer team member should pray that God will heal their woundedness, pray that He will cause His love, acceptance and forgiveness to become very real to them, and pray in the name of Jesus and in the power of the Holy Spirit to break any binding effect of those activities, vows or relationships which they have renounced. If you sense that something demonic has been attached to those issues that were just dealt with (and sometimes the Holy Spirit will reveal to you just exactly what is there) now is the time to rebuke it in the name of Jesus and demand that it leave.

The Lord works in many ways and every prayer ministry session is unique. Don't try to superimpose what happened when you were praying with one person, and make it what you expect to happen when you pray with someone else. Try to discern how God wants you to proceed in the particular session you are in at the time. The Lord may lead you to focus on a specific person in the individual's life and deal with all the issues involving that relationship. For example one session may focus on all the issues and all the things a person is holding against their father. Or the focus may be an event or the roots and issues involved in a habit such as overeating or pornography. With another person, He may lead you to start at the very beginning of their life and take things in chronological order as they occurred. He is a God of infinite variety.

When the person has no idea why they are the way they are or why they respond to things the way that they do, then we simply pray and ask Jesus, who does know, to reveal it to us. Often at this point the person will remember something that is a key which unlocks more when it is prayed over. Sometimes one of the prayer team members receives a word from the Lord or sees a picture in their mind and when they share it, it triggers the person's memory. And once in a while nobody has a clue! At this point agree to continue to intercede for the person between this session and the next one. Encourage them to pay attention during the next week to any persons or events that come to mind that they hadn't thought about for a long time.

Closing the Session

Always end the session with a prayer of blessing and the expressed desire that God would continue and protect the work that He is doing in the person's life. Thank Him and give Him the glory for what was accomplished that day.

You may feel led to give the person a suggestion of something specific to do during the time between your sessions. Some examples would be to ask them to continue praying over something very specific, or to keep a list of things God brings to mind. You might feel that the person would really benefit by getting some praise music and playing it at home or in their car. Maybe there is something that would be helpful for them to read. Maybe they need encouragement to get into the Word, or to find a church where they can fellowship, etc. We always want to encourage them to grow in their relationship with the Lord.

When the Season of Prayer Ministry is Over

The goal of healing prayer is for the person to become healthy in their heart, mind, spirit and body and for them to be able to continue on in their journey with the Lord. When healing comes, we release them to Him and bless them on their way, rejoicing in the work His Spirit has done.

Section 6: A Balanced Approach to Deliverance

Introduction to Deliverance

The seventy-two returned with joy and said, "Lord, even the demons submit to us in your name."
He replied, "I saw Satan fall like lightning from heaven. I have given you authority to trample
on snakes and scorpions and to overcome all the power of the enemy; nothing will harm you. How-
ever, do not rejoice that the spirits submit to you, but rejoice that your names are written in heaven."
Luke 10:18-20

The definition of deliverance is to liberate, to rescue, to set free, to send something to an intended target or destination. The responsibility to minister total healing and wholeness, which includes the ministry of deliverance, has been delegated to every Christian. We do this under the authority of Jesus and the Church and through the power of the Holy Spirit. We also do this with respect for the person. Deliverance is to be as orderly, loving and accepting as any other ministry to an individual. The goal is not simply to call upon God's power to fight and defeat the enemy; but to MINISTER THE LOVE OF JESUS.

Occasionally while ministering to someone a prayer minister will sense the presence of a demonic spirit. This spirit may manifest itself by voice changes, an evil look in the eyes, a sudden attitude change or in more dramatic ways, such as shouting, screaming, or violently shaking the individual. This can happen during prayer for someone for physical or inner healing or it can happen when a prayer minister walks into the room. The demon can have a violent reaction to the presence of the Holy Spirit within the prayer minister. We need to understand this is not abnormal, but a common reaction to God's power. Demons are spirit beings who are enemies of both God and Man and their reaction may be very strong if they sense that they are about to be confronted by Jesus.

Demons are enemies of the gifts and fruits of the Spirit. They keep the gifts from coming forth in the Christian's life. For example, the demon of resentment can have access to an individual because of unforgiveness. The person is unable to love others as they desire and they do not understand that a spiritual battle is being waged. Instead the person takes the blame and suffers in silence, wondering, "What is wrong with me?"

Demons are evil personalities. They are spirit beings who are enemies of God and man. There is not a person on this earth who escapes their notice. Satan and his cohorts devise plans to destroy each of us. First Peter 5:8 reminds us that Satan does not play fair. He is vigilant, especially when a person is vulnerable and weak. Satan does not give time off for illness or for good behavior. Satan hates you and wants to destroy you.

While some ministries are focused exclusively on deliverance, Wholeness Ministries views it as only a part of the ministry. We want to have a balanced approach in prayer ministry. We do believe that some people have stronger gifts in the area of deliverance just as some people have gifts that are stronger in other areas. We believe that God, who is the giver of all gifts, can and does give gifts at the time it is necessary, but as in any other area of ministry, we start as beginners and we learn and gain confidence with experience. Some deliverances from demonization can be difficult, so it is best for a new prayer minister to begin by observing this type of ministry, followed by times of ministering with a more experienced partner. If you find yourself in a situation you are not prepared to deal with, you close the prayer session with a prayer of protection and seek help and get the individual in touch with someone who can help. Remember, there are no emergencies in the Kingdom of God!

It is important for all of us to remember, at all times in this area of ministry, that God's power is greater than any demonic force and that we can walk in full obedience to the Lord's direction and not shrink back out of fear or a sense of inadequacy. Ultimately God is the deliverer. This is not a battle where the two forces are of equal strength. When demonic forces rage against a believer who understands their identity in Christ it is like a mosquito attacking the side of an elephant. Read again: Luke 4:18, Matthew 10:1 and Matthew 10:8. These scriptures are a clear mandate for this type of ministry. The Church has understood Jesus' Mandate from Isaiah 61 and Luke 4:18 to be its continuing Mandate. Part of this Mandate, very clearly, is to minister liberation to the captives.

Jesus' Mandate, and By Extension Ours:

The Spirit of the Lord is upon me, because he has anointed me to preach good news to the poor. He has sent me to proclaim freedom for the prisoners and recovery of sight to the blind, to release the oppressed, to proclaim the year of the Lord's favor. Luke 4:18

Jesus' Commission to Those Who Follow Him:

He called his twelve disciples to him and gave them authority to drive out evil spirits and to heal every disease and sickness. Matthew 10:1

Heal the sick, raise the dead, cleanse those who have leprosy, drive out demons. Freely you have received, freely give. Matthew 10:8

Definition of Deliverance Terms

Television shows and movies, as well as printed media, have contributed misunderstanding and confusion to the area of the demonic realm and deliverance ministry. For many people, this type of ministry seems to abandon reason and logic while embracing superstition and primitive culture. The thoughts of the person to whom you are ministering may vary from tremendous fear of even the term deliverance, to their being convinced that demons are just playful or mischievous elves that cannot do any real harm. In some cultures the devil is pictured as this harmless being that runs around in a red suit complete with a tail and pitchfork. There are those who believe that Christians cannot avoid demonic influence completely and those who believe that demons cannot be involved in a Christian's life at all. Be sensitive to the beliefs of the person and avoid further wounding or confusion by clearly understanding and carefully using correct terms and explaining as much as the person is ready to accept and understand.

Definition of Terms

1. OPPRESSION — The New Testament provides examples of demonic influence in people's lives such as Luke 6:18b: "Those troubled by evil spirits were cured. . . ." and Acts 5:16: "bringing their sick and those tormented by evil spirits, and all of them were healed." These verses describe demons who trouble, harass, afflict, or oppress people. OPPRESSION means "to keep under control by harsh and unjust use of force or authority, to lie heavily upon physically or mentally."

2. POSSESSION — Possession means "to be controlled by evil spirits; to enter, exert control over, dominate."

3. EXORCISM — A formal ceremony conducted to free a person possessed by evil spirits. In many denominations this formal prayer responsibility is assigned to specific people or must be approved by high officials in the church.

4. DELIVERANCE — A process of prayer for freeing a person who is oppressed by the demonic. A prayer for deliverance can also be a command directed to the oppressing demon(s). This command should be firm and authoritative, but it does not need to be shouted. Demons are not deaf! Acts 16:18 is an example of such a command spoken by Paul; "In the name of Jesus Christ I command you to come out of her!" More information on the prayer for deliverance is available later in this section.

Problems with the Term "Possession"

The problem for many Christians is in the term "possession". Real possession, when an individual's personality is submerged by an alien, evil force, is certainly rare. But the word in the New Testament which is often translated as "possessed" actually means, in the original Greek, "demonized" or "to have a demon" which is a much broader term. Though possession is rare, people who are "demonized," who are attacked or oppressed by demonic forces, are a relatively common occurrence. This is true even in the Christian community.

Can a Christian Be Demonized?

The answer to this question depends on our understanding of Body, Soul and Spirit. Theologians have debated whether man is made up of two parts or three parts for years. One school of thought says that the soul and spirit are one, not separate, and we are made up as two part beings, possessing a body and soul/spirit. Therefore, when an individual is reborn in Christ, both the soul and spirit are changed. Since the Holy Spirit is now living within them, there can be no oppression or influence (demonization) by the demonic realm. Evil spirits cannot abide in the same place with the Holy Spirit.

A second school of thought says that man is composed of a body, soul (containing mind, emotions and will) and spirit. This is where we in Wholeness Ministries stand.

> *May God himself, the God of peace, sanctify you through and through. May your whole spirit, soul and body be kept blameless at the coming of our Lord Jesus Christ. 1 Thessalonians 5:23*

When people give their lives to Jesus and become Christians a miracle takes place. A transfer of power and ownership is made. The person is rescued from the kingdom of the enemy. Jesus, the new ruler, places them in the Kingdom of God. The person's spirit is reborn, because Jesus won the right to do this by defeating Satan at the resurrection.

> *You, dear children, are from God and have overcome them, because the one who is in you is greater than the one who is in the world. 1 John 4:4*

However, we know that believers are not instantly conformed to the image of Jesus. Our sin nature is not eradicated when we accept Christ. Within the soul are areas which can allow demonic spirits to reside—anger, bitterness, rage, unforgiveness, etc. The Holy Spirit begins to help us on the path to sanctification.

> *For those God foreknew he also predestined to be conformed to the likeness of his Son, that he might be the firstborn among many brothers. Romans 8:29*

> *Do not conform any longer to the pattern of this world, but be transformed by the renewing of your mind. Then you will be able to test and approve what God's will is—his good, pleasing and perfect will. Romans 12:2*

When a demonized person comes to Christ, they experience a change of rulers in their spirit, but they do not attain complete freedom. A large percentage of demonized people will have become so prior to becoming Christians. Deliverance ministry is about bringing God's chosen and beloved children all of the freedom that Jesus desires to give. If a person is oppressed by evil spirits, then a prayer for deliverance is in order.

Indications That Deliverance is Needed

The people to whom we minister often have symptoms of deep psychological disturbance, which could also be interpreted as demonic interference. Since we cannot always verify the existence of demons with our physical eyes, it is important to use the other resources that God has given to indicate that deliverance is necessary. Setting out on deliverance ministry when that is not the need may further wound the person who has come for help.

The Interview

The interview may be non-existent in a situation where demonic manifestations erupt spontaneously in a ministry service. However, when possible, a separate interview session with a candidate for deliverance is ideal. This does not have to be a rigorous inquisition into past sins, but rather provides an opportunity to see if the person is open, honest and able to cooperate in the deliverance ministry. You also have the opportunity to observe any obvious symptoms of demonization, as described in the following sections.

Evil spirits come into a person's life for a reason. Charles Kraft identifies four of the most common ways that demons enter a person's life in his book <u>Deep Wounds, Deep Healing</u>.

- By invitation of the person or someone in authority over the person. An example would be a parent that has their child dedicated or given over to Satan.

- By inheritance from generation to generation.

- Through wrong reaction to emotional hurts. If you hold onto an emotion like anger it can turn into bitterness or rage and open the doorway to demonic harassment.

- Through sin. Habitual involvement in sin like drugs or pornography allows demonic spirits entrance, it gives them a right to be there.[1]

Sometimes it is due to sin on the part of the person and in other cases it is due to the sins of other people who had authority over the person. "Satan is a vicious legalist, and if any unconfessed sin is connected to the demonic infestation, the invading spirit will probably not leave when you pray, or else it may leave for a short time but will come right back and invade the area of the victim's weakness."[2]

The interview will help determine whether the person is aware of any sin in their life and whether they are ready to deal with it.

If the person is infested due to the sin of another, then forgiveness of the one who sinned against them will be needed to bring about deliverance. The interview can help determine what the person understands about forgiveness and whether they are able and willing to open themselves for this ministry.

In their pre-Christian days people can invite demons in through involvement in the occult. The offspring of those involved in the occult can also become demonized through inheritance. For more information on demonization as a result of occult activity see page 6-8. They can also invite demonic activity in their lives by getting involved with certain rock groups and their music, by committing an act or acts of sexual perversion, by playing games such as Dungeons and Dragons and through many other 'chosen' activities. During the interview process the person may describe a lifestyle that opened the way for this type of demonic infestation to occur. Their willingness to leave that lifestyle behind is a key to the future success of deliverance ministry.

The need for significant inner healing will usually be revealed during the interview. There are people who need inner healing who do not require deliverance, but people in need of deliverance always need some degree of inner healing. (See page 5-1 for a detailed description of inner healing.) "When people wallow in negative reactions to emotional wounds, they often get demonized."[3] Apparently when we retain negative reactions to abuse, such as unforgiveness, bitterness and anger, we weaken ourselves to the point that evil spirits can enter. Inner healing is the process that eliminates the things to which the demons can attach.

The interview is also a perfect opportunity to discuss how the prayer recipient can be preparing for ministry (See page 6-11) and to give them a Prayer Ministry Questionnaire (See page G-1), if that is appropriate. The preparation time can vary tremendously, from just a few days for those who have only some harassment to months for those who lead an unstable life that would leave the person open to immediate return of the demons.

If scheduling a separate session for the interview is unreasonable, then the interview can be completed at the first ministry session.

Identifying the Presence of Evil Spirits

There are several ways to find out that a person needs deliverance. Dr. Francis MacNutt, in his book Deliverance from Evil Spirits, gives sound counsel in this process of diagnosing spiritual illness. The following information is based on his material.

The Person Is Aware of Demonic Activity

The person in need of ministry often knows that the problem is being caused or exacerbated by evil spirits and will tell the prayer team. The person may hear voices that compel self destructive activity, such as "Drive off the road and into that tree." Others will hear voices that speak eternal condemnation, such as "You belong to me and will never escape." "You are condemned to hell forever." "You are not worthy to receive love."

Other people may have visions or nightmares that are more vivid than ordinary nightmares or feel the need to do things that they would never do under ordinary circumstances. The person knows that something is terribly wrong and senses some level of demonic oppression or control.

People who are genuinely afflicted by evil spirits usually are afraid to speak about the problem for fear that they will be written off as unbalanced or psychotic. While what they claim needs to be prayerfully evaluated, do not react with skepticism or scorn. Take what is claimed seriously and evaluate it with the help of the Holy Spirit, so that you do not further wound a hurting person.

You Observe Symptoms of Demonization

The person that you are interviewing or praying with may begin to act in a strange way that indicates the presence of one or more demons. Extreme examples include such things as the person trying to attack a prayer minister or slithering across the floor like a snake. Some of the more common signs follow.

- *Bodily Contortions* can indicate the presence of demonic activity. The New Testament describes these phenomena in Mark 1:26 and Mark 5:5: "The evil spirit shook the man violently" and "He would cry out and cut himself with stones." Body position will often reflect the active evil spirit; a spirit of pride or haughtiness may cause the person to assume a regal pose, while a spirit of fear may cause the person to pull his feet up on the chair and curl into a fetal position.

- *Voice Changes* that are sudden or unusual can indicate the presence of one or more evil spirits. The tone of voice changes can range from soft to husky or from mild-mannered to rude and insulting. The content can also change under the influence of an evil spirit. The person may start speaking in the plural, **WE** instead of **I**, begin speaking in a language they do not know, or say inappropriate things. Inappropriate remarks can range from insults and threats to sexual suggestions.

- *Facial Changes* may be very dramatic. Demonic activity can result in facial changes that differ from the person's normal expressions. The eyes of the person can be filled with hate, mockery, pride or whatever the nature of the active evil spirit. The eyes can roll so that only the white shows. Demons seem to be reluctant to have the person make eye contact with the prayer team. The entire face can be twisted with pain, anger or fear or any number of powerful responses.

- *Other Signs* of evil spirits can be demonstrated outside the person receiving ministry. An evil spirit may cause the room to grow cold or may notify you of its presence by an unpleasant smell. The spirit can also lull the person to sleep or into a state of total confusion.

Many of these signs associated with demonization can also result from psychological problems, so it is important to seek the guidance of the Holy Spirit before responding to observable symptoms.[4]

Discerning of Spirits

Deep personal problems can have a number of causes, such as the need to repent from sin, a chemical imbalance or physical problem that needs medical attention, verbal or physical abuse, the lack of love and care during childhood, oppression by demonic spirits, or a combination of several factors. The gift of discerning of spirits makes it possible to proceed into these delicate areas of ministry knowing God's plan for healing and freeing the person. This gift enables the prayer minister to know with assurance whether behavior is divine, human or satanic.

The apostle Peter apparently had this gift. He used it when he discerned that Satan had inspired Ananias to lie about his land sale, and Ananias was struck dead on the spot. He repeated this with Sapphira, who also died (see Acts 5:1-10). In this case the apparent generosity of Ananias and Sapphira seemed to be inspired by God, but it was actually a deception directed by Satan. The gift of discernment of spirits provides this kind of insight.

Deliverance needs to be ministered with caution and only after the Holy Spirit confirms that demonic activity is present, and that the Lord wants you to pray for this person at this time. God may reveal things to the prayer ministers for further intercession and fasting before it is time to minister to this area. Wait for God's leading and His timing.

> *If any of you lacks wisdom, he should ask God, who gives generously to all without finding fault, and it will be given to him. James 1:5*

The prayer team needs to be in agreement on the need for deliverance before continuing. If team members are sensing different ways to proceed, it may be time to end the session and have the team continue in intercession for wisdom and guidance. People do not fall prey to demons overnight and it is rarely necessary to treat deliverance as an emergency. Ministry to a suicidal person may be an exception to this. It is critical to rely on the guidance of the Holy Spirit. I repeat, there are no emergencies in the Kingdom of God!

If the person seeking ministry is not a Christian, the prayer team may want to delay deliverance ministry and give opportunity for the person to accept Jesus as their Savior. However, the process of experiencing God's freedom may cause the demonized person to turn to the Lord. (Romans 8: 35-36). Once again, listen to the Holy Spirit and follow His leading. Be aware that when you are leading a demonized person to the Lord there can be a lot of resistance and interference from evil spirits.

It is important to remember that when we are praying against demonic forces under the power and authority of Jesus Christ, we are ministering the mercy and compassion of Jesus to God's children. We must remember to see them as wounded people not evil beings, and to treat them with loving acceptance. Otherwise we may do far more harm than good in our ministry.

Occult Involvement

If the person coming for ministry has indicated on a Prayer Ministry Questionnaire (See page G-1) or in conversation that he or she has had involvement in any occult activity and this has not been dealt with in previous ministry, then deliverance may be needed. The Bible is very clear in forbidding all forms of fortune telling, witchcraft, spiritism, magic and involvement in false religious cults.

The following verses make it clear that there is no innocent involvement in the occult.

Exodus 22:18	Zechariah 10:2
Malachi 3:5	Leviticus 19:26, 31
Acts 8:9-13	Deuteronomy 18:9-13
Galatians 5:16-21	Isaiah 8:19, 47:13-14
Jeremiah 27:9-10	I Chronicles 10:13-14
Revelation 21:8, 22; 22:14-15	

Deuteronomy 18:9-13 is the command of Moses to the people on the eve of their entry into the Promised Land. Moses warns of the lure of satanic knowledge and power and then spells out the consequences of becoming involved in these pursuits in verse 12: "Anyone who does these things is detestable to the Lord..."

The level of a person's involvement in the occult needs to be considered. Francis MacNutt identifies the following five degrees of occult involvement:[5]

- *The unwitting entrance into Satan's kingdom* by engagement in spiritualism or other occult practices (e.g., playing the Ouija board) without intending to contact Satan

- *Knowingly seeking spiritual power to harm or dominate someone* by such practices as casting spells (e.g., going to a voodoo practitioner or witch because you seek success in love or want to curse an enemy)

- *Becoming a channel or witch,* allowing a spirit to take over part of your life (e.g., automatic writing)

- *Commencing a knowing, direct relationship with Satan* by making a pact with Satan

- *Becoming part of a coven engaged in Satan worship,* with the most severe levels of evil involving sexual orgies, torture, blood sacrifices (animal or human) and parodies of Christian worship

Those people who have unwittingly opened the door to the occult may have oppressing spirits, but even if they do not, the door needs to be closed by a positive action on the person's part. This door should be closed as soon as possible in the ministry time, so that the person is freed up to hear and receive from the Lord. Details on one way to close the door are provided on page 6-13, The Prayer of Deliverance.

Those people who have deliberately become involved in the occult are certain to require deliverance. The spirits may be more firmly attached and more difficult to eject as the level of the person's involvement in the occult increases. The Prayer Ministry Questionnaire provides several pages to help identify the degree of occult involvement. More preparation may be required of the person receiving ministry, especially if their involvement was long term, in order for them to fully cooperate with the deliverance and stay free when it is completed.

Preparing to Minister Deliverance

The ideal situation for deliverance ministry is for both the recipient and the team to have time to prepare in advance, though this may not always be possible. Prayer ministers and the prayer recipient need to seek the Lord in the days preceding the ministry time and to remain open to all that He wants to do. The time of preparation is as important as the actual ministry time. You may find, as the Lord uses you in more ways, that you need to stay prepared to minister at all times. You develop a lifestyle that honors and glorifies Him in all ways, you are sensitive to those needing ministry and you are a willing and able vessel.

Preparation of the Prayer Team

1. The prayer team members need to be selected with care and prayer. If an interview has been conducted, then information gained can be helpful in selecting a team. Each potential team member should examine themselves and be certain that they are entering the ministry session having been called by God to minister to this person at this time. A pure motive and a clean heart are a must for each team member.

2. Once selected, the team needs to spend time together in prayer for discernment and understanding of how to best minister to the individual. Unity among the team members is important. Each session is unique, so don't assume what worked with one person will work with others. Some deliverances can be completed in one session while others may require a series of appointments scheduled over several weeks.

3. Meditate on the power and authority available to those who minister in the name of Jesus. Praise God for who He is and His desire to bring freedom to the captives.

4. Select a location for the ministry time that is quiet, free of distractions and, ideally, under the control of your ministry group or church. Pray for God's chosen time to be revealed and for the cleansing of your chosen location.

5. Following deliverance, identify resources available to the person that will strengthen their walk with the Lord and have those ready to share.

6. Provide the team with a Prayer Ministry Questionnaire for the person they are praying for to complete prior to their first meeting, if this has not been done at an interview. See page G-1 for a sample Questionnaire. Have them answer as best as they can and return the Questionnaire to the team as soon as possible. Any questions about the Questionnaire can be reviewed at the first session.

7. Individual prayer and possibly fasting by each team member are also part of the preparation. Mark 9:29 is Jesus' response to his disciples when they asked why they had been unable to drive out an evil spirit: "He replied, 'This kind can come out only by prayer and fasting.'" Each team member needs to seek the guidance of the Holy Spirit on how to pray and how or whether to fast before praying for deliverance.

Knowing the Diversionary Tactics of the Enemy

Make certain that all team members are aware of the following types of diversionary tactics demons use prior to and during a ministry session and teach them how to pray to stop these tactics:

1. Demonic spirits will try to convince the person coming for ministry to cancel the session or frighten them into skipping it. It is not uncommon to receive a call prior to the session from the individual coming for ministry. They will often say they are feeling ill or something else has come up preventing them from coming at that time. Reassure them that this is a normal occurrence, pray for their protection and resolve. Provide encouraging scripture for the person to read daily prior to the ministry session.

2. Demonic spirits may scream, plead, bargain, threaten or cause confusion to try and make you give up. Pray for the Holy Spirit to take control and forbid all showy and disruptive behavior.

3. Demons may cause the people in the session to become sleepy or try to prevent speech or hearing in order to confuse. Pray for the mind of Christ for each person, for clarity and for focus on the work that God wants to do.

4. Demons may mock the prayer team. "You don't know what you are doing." "Who do you think you are?" Remind the demons that you are a child of God, purchased with the blood of Jesus, and you come in His authority.

Demons gain much of their power via bluffing and deception. They use these diversionary tactics to cause fear, confusion, disruption and discouragement, so that the deliverance session will stop. The prayer team needs to be constantly aware that God's power far exceeds that of our enemy. They also need to pray specific prayers of guidance and protection, before the session begins. The team needs to respond to the evil spirits with authority, but it is not necessary to speak in either a loud or angry voice, since this may confuse or wound the person receiving prayer.

Preparation of the Prayer Recipient

The following preparation should be suggested to the Prayer Recipient in advance of the ministry time:

1. Spend time reading the Bible each day. Meditate on encouraging verses. Also spend time being quiet and waiting on God.

2. Attend church and get involved in opportunities for fellowship with other Christians.

3. Listen to praise music, especially songs that are based on scripture.

4. Ask God to prepare you to receive all that He wants to do for you. Ask Him to show you specific things that He wants to deal with during ministry.

5. Be aware that you may feel discouraged or hopeless, thinking that ministry will not change anything. The enemy comes in to try to stop people from learning the truth of God's love and healing. If this hopelessness gets too great, contact someone from your ministry team so that they can pray with you on the telephone.

6. Complete the Prayer Ministry Questionnaire provided as carefully as possible, but do not worry about those questions that you cannot answer or do not understand. Ask the team about these items at the first session. Send the Questionnaire to the designated person as soon as possible.

You may wish to add other items to this list or to be very specific in the Scripture you ask them to read. If so, preparation instructions may need to be given in writing.

The Deliverance Prayer Session

All prayer ministry is to minister the love, mercy and compassion of Jesus to God's children. The deliverance prayer session is no exception. You must remember at all times that the person is wounded and in pain, even when evil beings speak and act through them. Be certain that the person understands that your firm commands directed to the demons are not an expression of anger toward them. You may need to remind them of this several times as you proceed through the ministry time.

Prayers for Guidance and Protection

Once introductions are made and the prayer recipient is comfortably settled, the team should open with prayer. A model prayer developed by Christian Healing Ministries, Jacksonville, FL is included on page I-1. This prayer can be used to open a session for an individual or for a group ministry time. You can also pray your own words, but the prayer should include the following elements:

1. Pray for protection. Pray under the power and authority of the blood of Christ. The name of Jesus and the Word of God are powerful weapons of prayer. Use scripture in your prayers as you are led by the Holy Spirit and use the name of Jesus with reverence, authority and faith. Pray that Christ's protection surround each person in the room and their families and friends from any retaliation by demonic forces. Forbid them to cause any harm or physical disturbance. Put on the whole armor of God (Ephesians 6:10-18).

2. Pray that the power of the Holy Spirit fill the room and provide guidance and discernment. Ask for the Holy Spirit to anoint with power and the love of God to heal as well as deliver. Loose the Holy Spirit to do all that He wants to accomplish and submit yourself to the Lordship of Jesus, recognizing that it is not the team members who bring deliverance, but it is God who does the work.

3. Forbid the demonic spirits to communicate with other spirits either inside or outside of the person. Forbid them to manifest in any way by shouting, violence, physical disruption or showy behavior. Forbid them to find refuge in any other person.

Identifying the Evil Spirits

It can be very helpful to find out the identity of the demon you are driving out. This can happen in several ways:

1. The person doing the praying or one of the team members knows through discernment of spirits what the demon is.

2. The person being prayed for knows who the demon is.

3. Through the interviewing process and/or the completed Prayer Ministry Questionnaire you have been able to discern the characteristic activity of the demon. Demons can have function names. An example would be a spirit of rage or anger. His function would be to manifest this emotion; therefore, speak to the spirit of rage and command it to leave.

It is not absolutely essential that you know the name of the demon in order to drive it out but it helps in identifying with what you are dealing. Ask the Holy Spirit to identify any area of demonic oppression and to help decide the priority in which they should be cast out. It may be helpful to have one team member write down the spirits that are identified and to make any notes of direction from the Lord as to priority or technique. The Holy Spirit is faithful to guide and direct a session if we continually submit ourselves to His direction.

You need to be aware of evil spirits who have as their function the protection of other demons. Spirits such as mockery, lying and confusion fit this category. These spirits will need to be eliminated first, or at the very least commanded to be silent, in order to reach the major spirit or spirits. More powerful demons will sacrifice those that are weaker in order to hide and avoid leaving.

During the prayer time ask the person receiving ministry to tell you what they hear in their head. Evil spirits will often talk to them in order to scare them, so that they will discontinue ministry. As they report what is going on in their mind, it can be dealt with through prayers of command.

Deliverance and Inner Healing

When praying for deliverance we have found without exception there is always a need for inner healing. This could be as a result of something the person did or something that was done to them. In any case it must be dealt with and usually involves both repentance and forgiveness. If this is not dealt with chances are the demonic forces will refuse to leave or return because they still have a foothold.

As demons are identified, then you need to determine whether there is unconfessed sin involved. If so, ask the person to renounce any sin connected with it and repent of that sin. At this point there may also be a need for some inner healing ministry, especially in the area of forgiveness. See page 5-1 for a detailed description of the inner healing and forgiveness ministry.

For those people who have experienced severe abuse, especially as part of rituals, and for those who have been heavily involved in the occult, it may be necessary to do some extensive inner healing work before any deliverance can proceed. The person may also need to further prepare for ministry by following the disciplines recommended for staying free on page 6-19, Responsibilities of the Liberated. Personal discipleship may be needed to get them through the process.

The Prayer of Deliverance

The door to any occult activity that has been part of the person's life needs to be closed prior to the actual deliverance prayer. The first step is to repent of every act committed that has led to an involvement with the occult. Even if the act was done out of a certain innocence, such as palm reading at a teenage slumber party, the person needs to ask God's forgiveness and turn from sin. They can use a simple prayer such as the one that follows.

> *Lord, I did not know what I was doing, but now I realize I should not have _____.*
> *I am sorry that I did and I ask your forgiveness.*

The second step is to renounce the occult involvement. In repenting, you tell God that you are sorry, turn away from the sin, and with the help of God, decide to stay on the right path. Renouncing goes a step further in that you actively turn against the sin and the occult. This can be done with the following simple statement.

> *I renounce _____ and any involvement in the occult that I had through this*
> *activity.*

An important element of renunciation is the willingness to eliminate books and objects connected with occult involvement. Burning is the classic way to destroy these items, but the person should evaluate their circumstances and eliminate them in an appropriate way. These items should not be given to other people.[6]

> *A number who had practiced sorcery brought their scrolls together and burned them publicly.*
> *When they calculated the value of the scrolls, the total came to fifty thousand drachmas. Acts 19:19*

Once the demons are identified and God's plan has been discerned, the actual prayer for deliverance can be very simple. The wording can vary, but should include the following:

> *In the name of Jesus Christ I bind you and command you, spirit of_____, to leave*
> *without causing harm or disturbance. I break your power over_____ and send you to*
> *the feet of Jesus Christ. Now go!*

You notice that this prayer of deliverance has several components.

- The name of Jesus, which provides the authority for deliverance, must be used with reverence, authority and faith.

- The name or function of the demon being commanded to go, as identified in interview and intercession is clearly stated.

- The command itself - what to do, where to go, how to go - is spoken with authority.

This prayer should be spoken in a firm voice, but it need not be shouted. The dignity of the person needs to be maintained at all times; the ministry time should not further wound or confuse them. Always remember that the person is God's child.

Often the prayer team can see the demon leave by the body language of the person being prayed for. Often the person receiving deliverance knows when the demon is gone and will tell you. Sometimes you can see a terrific struggle going on internally and then a sudden relaxing when the spirit departs. If the spirit does not depart, then some additional inner healing and/or forgiveness issues may need to be dealt with or some additional intercession may need to occur. Seek the guidance of the Holy Spirit before proceeding. If there are multiple spirits to be dealt with, proceed as the Spirit leads, taking note of the physical and mental condition of the individual. Take breaks if you need to do so and be considerate of the time frame the ministry recipient has available.

This prayer time should also include filling the emptiness created by the departing demons with the Holy Spirit. Forbid the demons to return and request that the love of God and the power of the Holy Spirit fill the person to overflowing. Bless them with all the fruit of the Spirit and pray for their protection and their strengthening to stand against the enemy when he tries to convince them that nothing really happened.

Responsibilities of the Liberated

Deliverance is a walk, not a once and for all experience without any responsibility on the part of the person who has been set free. To remain free from any additional demonic influence, a person must choose to turn and begin walking in the Spirit. The individual must stop any behavior which allowed the demons a foothold; this happens only through the Holy Spirit's work in their lives. The freed person also needs a support system, especially when they feel weak and in danger of succumbing to temptation again. The areas previously occupied by evil need to be continually filled with the good things of God.

Study and Meditate on the Scripture.

Strengthen your faith with passages on deliverance, protection and the power of Jesus' name and His blood, such as:

Psalm 91	Mark 16:17
Exodus 12:23	Romans 8:28-30
Luke 10:17	Ephesians 2:6;6:10
Isaiah 54:17	John 10:27-29
Revelation 12:11	

Jack Hayford, in his book The Power and Blessing, describes some of his own difficulties in establishing this habit until he established one simple rule, "I simply don't turn out the light. That's right. I've connected that last action of the day to becoming 'impossible' without reading the Word."[7]

The freed person should be encouraged in both personal Scripture reading and meditation and corporate study. Prayer team members need to be aware of good sources of nourishment for those with whom they pray. Every Christian needs to feed on truth to grow, but it is critical for the newly freed.

> *Then you will know the truth, and the truth will set you free. John 8:32*

Prayer

The newly freed person needs to pray and ask God for the heart-desire and discipline to develop a consistent prayer life. Praying in their native language and/or prayer language will help them abide in the love of God.

> *Then Jesus told his disciples a parable to show them that they should always pray and not give up. Luke 18:1*

> *But you, dear friends, build yourselves up in your most holy faith and pray in the Holy Spirit. Jude 20*

Learning to pray according to the prompting of the Holy Spirit and with the power of the Spirit will bless the person in their new freedom and help them remain free. Asking the Spirit to flood their life each day brings the power to resist

Praise

An attitude of praise and thanksgiving is another powerful way to remain free of evil spirits. Giving praise when the enemy attacks puts the focus on God, rather than on the enemy. The enemy does not want to produce this response, and he will flee (James 4:7,8). Read more about praise as a weapon of spiritual warfare on page 7-22.

Wait on God

One of the most difficult disciplines we must learn is to wait in silence and solitude on God. Our minds are often so busy and preoccupied with tasks that need to be done that we find it impossible to quietly sit in the presence of God, receiving from Him and enjoying being with Him. This is often when we discover how valuable we are to Him. That we are His beloved. That knowledge is a powerful weapon in our walk to stay free from demonic influence.

Renew the Mind and Resist

Often the person coming out of demonic oppression has an area of weakness or sin that opened them up to the demonic activity in the first place. Even if the evil spirits came as a result of someone else's sinful activity, long term exposure to evil spirits and their lies usually results in areas of weakness. Although the mind of Christ has been given to every believer and enables each one to evaluate their thoughts, the mind tends to dwell on worldly thoughts rather than on God's truth. The newly freed person needs to be taught the following steps for renewing the mind so that their thoughts line up with God's Word and then their emotions and actions will come into line with the truths of God.

1. Ask the Holy Spirit to reveal thoughts and thought patterns that need to be changed and renewed. The believer is commanded to renew their thought life in Romans 12:2, because all sin originates in one's thoughts. Many of our painful emotions (fear, anger, tension) are often the product of believing Satan's lies.

2. Ask the Holy Spirit to surface the root memories of events where the wrong thought was strongly reinforced.

3. If the root memory involved hurting or wounding by another person, chose to forgive that person. See page 5-11 for more on forgiveness.

4. Discover what God says in the Bible concerning the particular false belief or lie that one has believed and argue against it with the truth of God's Word.

5. Replace the lie of that wrong thinking with the truth of God's Word.

   • Memorize applicable scripture

- Meditate on the truth

- Personalize scripture, putting it in the first person

- Confess the scripture aloud when tempted to embrace the enemy's lie

Sometimes the newly freed person still has a vague sense of worthlessness after the deliverance. The lie says, "I am not worthy of God's love or anyone else's love either." The lie may have come in due to comments and attitudes of parents or a teacher. After identifying the source(s), the individual needs to forgive those people who spoke the lie and then take a scripture like 1 John 4:9-11 that speaks of God's love and the sacrificial death of Jesus as a result of that great love. As the newly freed person meditates on these words, they can say to these thoughts of worthlessness, "I have great worth because God loves me so much that He gave His son's life for me." Over time, with the Holy Spirit working in their life, the mind is renewed. Truth replaces the lie of the enemy.

Fellowship

Growth in the Christian walk is an essential aspect of remaining free. The person who is trying to remain free of evil spirits needs to avoid, when possible, the people and places that brought about or contributed to their oppression. This may not be possible if, for example, it is a spouse, a parent or a sibling that is involved in the occult. The freed person must diligently seek the Lord on what to do in such a case.

Breaking away from damaging relationships can leave the person alone and vulnerable. Fellowship in the Body of Christ can help alleviate loneliness while providing opportunities for discipline and encouragement in the new walk with the Lord. Acts 2:42-47 describes an ideal fellowship of believers that resulted in personal growth and healing, as well as corporate growth.

The church and its small groups also provide opportunities to confess struggles and share victories with fellow believers. Ideally someone in the group will be able to give guidance on how to counteract areas of weakness and grow in the Lord and the group will provide love and acceptance that was not available with those people involved in the oppressive activities.

Follow-up Appointments

When the ministry session or sessions have been completed, offer the person the opportunity to call for a follow-up appointment in a few weeks. The person will often realize that there is something else to be addressed in the days following ministry, or they will realize that their spiritual weapons need to be sharpened. Knowing that they are welcome to call for additional help is usually very encouraging to the ministry recipient.

Section 7: Spiritual Warfare

Origin and Purpose of Spiritual Warfare

Like many other areas in Christianity, spiritual warfare is in great need of balance. People tend toward two extremes: overemphasis or under-emphasis. Those who overemphasize spiritual warfare see demons in everything. With them, every problem is solved by casting out a demon. Those who underemphasize spiritual warfare are convinced that if they think or talk about the enemy, they will become vulnerable to his attacks. They focus on the victory won by Jesus at the cross and ignore the possiblity that we are even in a war. Understand this, if you are a believer, whether you like or not, you are in spiritual warfare. You are either in it actively or passively.

When we become aware of a war the first thing we find out is the identity of the adversaries. We know that our adversaries are Satan and his demonic hordes. A natural question then follows. What are they fighting over?

First Decisive Choice

To understand spiritual warfare we must start at the very beginning. The first words in Genesis are "In the beginning God created the heavens and the earth." When God created angelic beings He gave them a free will, an ability to choose allegiance to God or opposition to Him. Lucifer (Satan) became prideful and desired to be like God. Out of that desire he chose to rebel against God. The creation can never be as great or greater than the Creator and thus Satan's efforts were futile. God could have destroyed Satan and his rebels at that very moment but He chose not to do so. Instead He expelled them from heaven.

Second Decisive Choice

This took place in the Garden of Eden with Satan deceiving Adam and Eve. Both Adam and Eve chose to disobey God which then gave Satan authority over all the earth. Man was created for an intimate relationship with God. Satan was jealous of that relationship and of an ability God gave man that He did not give angelic beings, procreation. From then on the battle has been over mankind. Satan, out of his jealousy, is fighting to deprive God of His relationship with man. He uses all of his evil abilities to keep us from that intimacy. God, on the other hand offers us an opportunity to have an intimate relationship with Him. He calls us His Beloved and makes it very clear in Scripture that we are the crown of His creation and that He created us for relationship. These, then, are the two sides of the battle.

In looking at these two choices we see God's restraint in eliminating evil, which, being God, He easily could have done. We see evil remaining in creation because the presence of free will is more valuable to God than its absence. God tolerates evil in creation so that we continue to have a free will. "God has chosen to deal with evil through man's free will, not in spite of it."[1]

God is sovereign. He is capable of doing anything, even working out His will through evil and our imperfect choices.

And we know that in all things God works for the good of those who love him, who have been called according to his purpose. Romans 8:28

This verse applies not only to each of us individually but to mankind corporately. In essence God is saying to us, "Your free will is much more important to me than the evil you have allowed in. Therefore, I will use it for your good."

In being victorious at the cross (Hebrews 3:14), Christ has already won the battle with Satan. Why then is a defeated Satan still on the loose?

It has been God's purpose from the beginning of the universe that His Son, Jesus Christ, should have a bride (Revelation 19:7) to share his throne for eternity. Christ came for the specific purpose of creating the universal Church, His Body of whom He is Head.

I pray that the eyes of your heart may be enlightened, so that you may know what is the hope of his calling, what are the riches of the glory of His inheritance in the saints, and what is the surpassing greatness of his power toward us who believe. These are in accordance with the working of the strength of his might which he brought about in Christ when he raised him from the dead, and seated him at his right hand in the heavenly places, far above all rule and authority and power and dominion and every name that is named, not only in this age, but also in the one to come. And he put all things in subjection under his feet, and gave him as head over all things to the church, which is his body, the fullness of him who fills all in all. Ephesians 1:18-23

When we receive salvation we become part of that body. We are a body in training to become a bride who co-rules the universe with her Bridegroom (Revelation 3:21). "Everything God has done since the beginning of creation is for this purpose."[2]

God is sovereign (Psalm 103:19). There is nothing that is not under His authority, even Satan. Although he is defeated, Satan has been allowed to be active for the specific task of participating in our training. God is actually using Satan for His own purposes. Christ has already overcome and we must be trained to overcome also so that we are a bride ready for her Bridegroom. I heard Dean Sherman say, "If we are going to be overcomers we must have something to overcome. This includes those things which we consider uncomfortable, painful, evil and opposed to what we want in our lives. "We would love to have a life free of rough spots and pain but that is not how we learn best. It is often through adversity that we learn about God and submit to Him."[3]

Overcoming Adversity

Spiritual warfare and God's training are illustrated in the life of Joseph. We know from the story of Joseph beginning in Genesis 39 that what happened to Joseph was meant to destroy him. At 17 Joseph was sold into slavery by his brothers. It was not until he was 39 that he would see his family again. For 13 of those years he was under God's intense training until he had those "Christlike" qualities that could be used by God. They were years of both favor and adversity. He was sold to Potiphar in Egypt and found favor in his household. However, after being wrongly accused by Potiphar's wife he wound up in prison. After finding favor with Pharaoh by interpreting his dreams,

Joseph became second in authority only to Pharaoh. In this capacity he was able to aid his family in time of famine when they came to Egypt to buy food.

As Joseph addresses his brothers we see the outcome of spiritual warfare and the results of God's training. Joseph had two choices concerning how he would react to his circumstances. He could have become bitter, resentful, angry and full of hate toward God. This was the result Satan was working to accomplish. However, as he talks with his brothers it is obvious that he made another choice.

> *But God sent me ahead of you to preserve for you a remnant on earth and to save your lives by a great deliverance. So then, it was not you who sent me here, but God. He made me father to Pharaoh, lord of his entire household and ruler of all Egypt Genesis 45:7,8*

Joseph chose to see God's sovereignty in all of his life, not just in the good things but in the adversity as well. Satan lost the battle to alienate Joseph from God. God changed Joseph's character in circumstances of adversity so that he could be used to save the rest of his family. We often have the same choice; to side with Satan and be alienated from God or to side with God and allow Him, in all circumstances, to change us into the image of His Son.

Earlier I said, each one of us is in the midst of our own spiritual warfare: ". . . some of us may never actually initiate spiritual warfare, but all of us must face the fact that the devil has initiated warfare against us."[4] This is the training ground for our eternal work. God gave man a free will just as He did the angels. Satan cannot and God will not normally violate our free will. Therefore, we choose, either consciously or unconsciously, whose side we will be on. For the most part we think of "the enemy" as Satan, but often we are our own worst enemy. The "Flesh" is that fallen part of us which we inherited from Adam and Eve. It is the part of us that operates outside of God's power and authority. Not only does the Flesh get us in trouble it readily agrees with Satan just as Adam and Eve did. Satan attacks this weak part of us. The "World" is the fallen part of creation which also influences the Flesh. When we succumb to Satan's suggestions or the influence of the World we cannot blame them, for we are responsible for our own choices.

All of Life

Spiritual warfare involves absolutely every aspect of our lives. At stake is our becoming Christlike. Christlikeness is key to a growing relationship with God. To become more Christlike we must enter the warfare. Choosing not to enter into spiritual warfare puts us squarely on Satan's side in this battle. Instead of becoming Christlike we are taking on Satan's qualities. "This is war, and there is no neutral ground. If you're not on my side, you're the enemy; if you're not helping, you're making things worse"[5.] The "Good News" of spiritual warfare is that the battle is not ours but God's (1 Samuel 17:47, 2 Chronicles 20:15). Our part is to choose God's side, submit to Him and be obedient. When we give God permission in this way He is free to do His work in us, to conform us to the image of His Son (Romans 8:29).

Be prepared for Satan's opposition when you enter spiritual warfare. His goal is to separate you from God. He does not play fair and will throw all sorts of obstacles and deceptions in your pathway. You will be learning from Satan as well as from God but your eyes should be on God. Do not allow Satan to use information about himself to instill a fear of him or in any way draw your attention away from God. You need to be knowledgeable concerning Satan but <u>focused on God at all times</u>.

Knowing God and the Enemy

Strategy is an extremely important element in warfare. We need to know the nature of God and Satan, what they are trying to accomplish with us and the strategy they use to accomplish that end. How do we do this? We get to know both God and Satan. The Bible is God's textbook on Himself as well as Satan. The Word is Truth.

An important element in spiritual warfare is balance in our perspective of it. If we are to study Satan and his tactics we must also study God at the same time. To study one to the exclusion of the other leads to imbalance. To study neither leads to total ignorance. Ignorance is not bliss, ignorance is darkness and Satan operates in darkness. One of his most effective strategies has been to keep the Church in ignorance. Jesus says in John 8:31-32, "... If you hold to my teaching, you are really my disciples. Then you will know the truth, and the truth will set you free." This includes setting us free from what Satan would do to us by knowing what he is up to. We must be "aware of but not impressed by him."[6] Satan's nature is to intimidate and impress and if we know the Truth we will not succumb to either one.

Knowing God

Knowing God starts with our own hearts. The heart is the place of our emotions, our moral side and our will as opposed to our intellectual side. First Corinthians 3:18-19 says, "Do not deceive yourselves. If any one of you thinks he is wise by the standards of this age, he should become a 'fool' so that he may become wise. For the wisdom of this world is foolishness in God's sight."

> *The man without the Spirit does not accept the things that come from the Spirit of God, for they are foolishness to him, and he cannot understand them, because they are spiritually discerned. 1 Corinthians 2:14*

God sees the things of this world as foolishness but our intellectual side sees them as wise. The intellectual side of us perceives God's Truth as foolishness. God's Kingdom is backward to fallen human nature. This is divine logic versus fallen human logic. If we desire to know God we must set aside our human logic and come to Him with surrendered hearts. Our wills must be bent to searching for Him.

> *"You will seek me and find me when you seek me with all your heart. I will be found by you," declares the Lord . . . Jeremiah 29:13-14*

God does not fight for our attention. We must choose to do the seeking because He gave us a free will.

God makes Himself easily found when we search in the right place. Second Corinthians 5:7 says, "We live by faith, not by sight. . . ." And what is faith? "Now faith is being sure of what we hope for and certain of what we do not see" (Hebrews 11:1). Our intellectual side wants to find God in creation, in the physical and do it with our own logic. Evidence of God's hand can easily be found in creation and we can connect with God both intellectually and spiritually through His creation.

For since the creation of the world God's invisible qualities - his eternal power and divine nature - have been clearly seen, being understood from what has been made, so that men are without excuse. Romans 1:20

We can learn about God from creation. But God Himself is a spirit and is not found in the physical realm but in the spiritual realm. "So we fix our eyes not on what is seen, but on what is unseen. For what is seen is temporary, but what is unseen is eternal" (2 Corinthians 4:18). If we are to find God we must search the spiritual realm with our hearts of faith, accepting by faith that God's Word is Truth. We cannot understand God on our own because our "natural man" cannot understand the things of God. The Holy Spirit is our only teacher. "We have not received the spirit of the world but the Spirit who is from God, that we may understand what God has freely given us" (1 Corinthians 2:12).

Some of my most treasured times are those when I get away to a canyon near my home. There is a raging river flowing through this canyon and I often go and sit there for hours doing absolutely nothing. Since I am a part of God's creation I feel as if I connect with God through nature. These are intimate times when I sometimes sing, dance, swim, sit still, pray, laugh and even nap.

Since the fall in the Garden of Eden God's purpose has been to restore us to the relationship He intended us to have with Him from the very beginning. That relationship is both now and in eternity. Absolutely everything God does is towards that end. We, therefore, must have a realistic view of God as He reveals Himself in the Word.

Knowing the Enemy

Knowing the enemy starts with taking God at His Word, that there indeed is an enemy (John 10:10). Many eliminate spiritual warfare in their own minds by denying Satan's tactics. It is dangerous to ignore God's Word especially where Satan is concerned. All we <u>need</u> to know about Satan comes from God, either through His Word or by revelation.

Satan is our adversary. He is deceptive, a slanderer, a murderer, a liar, a destroyer, evil, the "Prince of this world", our tempter, "god of this age", "Prince of the power of the air", accuser, manipulative, and divisive. All of Satan's tactics are designed to separate us from God in one way or another by attacking the character and glory of God. He whispers, "Is He really who He says He is?" "If He were really good and omnipotent He would not allow adversity in our lives." "God couldn't possibly love me the way I am." All of these thoughts and more Satan can speak to us. We must learn to recognize their source and falsehood. Satan's tactics are tailor-made for us. He and his army spend time getting to know us just like very good friends or spouses do. He reads our words and actions and then fashions his tactics just for us and our circumstances. Satan and his army are very experienced. They've had thousands of years to learn about human nature and to hone their skills.
Despite Satan's wide ranging powers and tactics he does have limitations.

1. Satan cannot penetrate the Blood of Jesus (Exodus 12, Revelation 12:11).

2. Satan cannot read your mind. (Case in point - Satan misread Job.) Satan is a created being and so is not omniscient, omnipresent or omnipotent. However, he can read your words and actions just as people can.

3. Satan cannot confess Jesus Christ as Lord or acknowledge the saving work of Jesus (1 Corinthians 12:3, 1 John 4:2-3).

4. Satan has limits. God is sovereign and as such has limited Satan's realm of authority. We see this when Satan approaches God for permission to do what he wanted to Job (Job 1:12, 2:6) and Peter (Luke 22:31-32). Satan must get permission to do whatever is outside of his realm. Even within his realm the conditions for an encounter are set by God. Satan cannot stop God's ultimate purposes from coming to pass. Satan's destiny is sure (Psalm 103:19).

5. Satan is silenced by praise (Psalm 8:2). God inhabits the praises of His people. God and Satan cannot coexist and so Satan flees.[7]

These limitations are the basis for some of our weapons and tactics against Satan which are discussed on page 7-12 and following.

The Occult

Pride was the sin that caused Satan to regard himself more highly than God. It is that same pride and a lust for power that is the root sin of the occult. Instead of seeking God's power in their lives, those who become involved in the occult have made the choice to take control of their own lives. They have been deceived into thinking they have power and can control their own destiny. The truth is they are under the control of demonic powers whose purpose is to "steal, kill and destroy". See page 6-8 and following for more on the occult.

I remember very cleary on one of my trips overseas having a conversation with a young girl who was heavily involved in Satan worship. At one one point I said to her, "You know that he only wants to destroy you," and she replied, "yes, I know." "Then why, I asked, would you want to follow him?" She replied, "because he gives me power!'

The Battleground

It is most important that we understand where the war is taking place. The battle and its location are described in the following verse.

> *For though we live in the world, we do not wage war as the world does. The weapons we fight with are not the weapons of the world. On the contrary, they have divine power to demolish strongholds. We demolish arguments and every pretension that sets itself up against the knowledge of God, and we take captive every thought to make it obedient to Christ. 2 Corinthians 10:3-5*

Our mind is the battlefield. It does not matter at what level Satan's attacks come, the reality is the attack is aimed at our mind. For example, we may be in a horrendous traffic accident which results in numerous injuries, hospitalization, and permanent disabilities. Or perhaps a young child dies. The attack came at a physical level but was aimed at our minds. Will this attack separate us from God as Satan hopes or strengthen us in faith and character as God intends? Will we believe Satan's subtle urging that if God were really good and loving He would not allow this to happen to us? Or will we believe God when the Word says, "And we know that in all things God works for the good of those who love him, who have been called according to his purpose" (Romans 8:28)? We have a choice and with that choice we win or lose the battle.

Spiritual Warfare Is One Choice After Another

Winning the spiritual warfare battle is a matter of choice. It is choosing the winning side, time after time after time after time. Do we choose the things of God or the enemy? In Joshua 24:15 Joshua challenges Israel to a choice, "But if serving the Lord seems undesirable to you, then choose for yourselves this day whom you will serve, whether the gods your forefathers served beyond the River, or the gods of the Amorites, in whose land you are living. But as for me and my household, we will serve the Lord". We live in the land of the enemy and we must constantly choose between the Lord or the gods of this world. Ultimately the choice comes down to choosing and serving God or "self".

Blessings and Curses

We live under a system of blessings and curses instituted by God in this less than perfect world. "This day I call heaven and earth as witnesses against you that I have set before you life and death, blessings and curses. Now choose life, so that you and your children may live and that you may love the Lord your God, listen to His voice, and hold fast to Him. For the Lord is your life, and He will give you many years in the land He swore to give to your fathers, Abraham, Isaac and Jacob" (Deuteronomy 30:19-20). Blessing and cursing are invoked by God and man. In both cases, blessing is the result of obedience and cursing of disobedience to God. All creation comes under this system.

In all areas of our lives we must maintain a balanced view of God. God is not beyond bringing judgment on the disobedient and ungodly. Paul stresses this balanced view to the Romans.

> *Consider therefore the kindness and sternness of God; sternness to those who fell, but kindness to you, provided that you continue in his kindness. Romans 11:22*

God is not all sternness or kindness. He dispenses both.

In Deuteronomy 28, Moses outlines the blessings and curses which God put into effect. These can be used as a measurement, both on a personal and corporate level, as to which we come under. Summarized, they look like this.

Blessing	Curse
Exaltation	Humiliation
Health	Barrenness
Reproductiveness	Unfruitfulness
Prosperity	Mental and physical sickness

Victory	Family breakdown
God's favor	Poverty
	Defeat
	Oppression
	Failure
	God's disfavor[8]

As the only Judge, God gives us the rewards for obedience and the punishments for disobedience. It is God's strategy for nudging us toward Him. If we come under God's curse, it is by ignorance of God's laws. We are responsible for our sin whether we know God's laws or not. Psalm 119:173,174 expresses David's appreciation of God's laws and ways. ". . . I have chosen your precepts, I long for your salvation, O Lord, and your law is my delight".

Blessings and curses also proceed from man. God would have us dispense only blessings, both to ourselves and to others. Romans 12:14 says "bless and do not curse". When we choose to curse instead of bless we are actually standing in judgment, both of others and of God's law.

> *Brothers, do not slander one another. Anyone who speaks against his brother or judges him speaks against the law and judges it. When you judge the law, you are not keeping it, but sitting in judgment on it. There is only one Lawgiver and Judge, the one who is able to save and destroy. But you - who are you to judge your neighbor? James 4:11,12*

The most common agent by which blessing and curses are invoked is words. These may be spoken aloud, written or uttered inwardly. Proverbs 18:21 states, "The tongue has the power of life and death . . ." James emphasized the power which such a small aspect of our bodies has.

> *Consider what a great forest is set on fire by a small spark. The tongue also is a fire, a world of evil among the parts of the body. It corrupts the whole person, sets the whole course of his life on fire, and is itself set on fire by hell. All kinds of animals, birds, reptiles and creatures of the sea are being tamed and have been tamed by man, but no man can tame the tongue. It is a restless evil, full of deadly poison. With the tongue we praise our Lord and Father, and with it we curse men, who have been made in God's likeness. Out of the same mouth come praise and cursing. My brothers, this should not be James 3:5-10*

As Christians we have a responsibility to be aware of the blessing and curse system and to make the choice to stay in God's blessing and dispense only blessing to others, both friend and foe. Authority carries a responsibility for those under that authority. In the family, the authority passes from God to husband, parent to child. Wives and children are subject to the blessings and curses the husband and father brings to the family. If the family authority is living in disobedience, the whole family is subject to the consequences. In the church, the authority passes from God to senior pastor, to pastoral staff, to leadership, to congregation. The body of each church functions under blessing or curse according to the actions of those in authority. In schools teachers have authority over children and the power to bless or curse. In jobs bosses have this same authority over employees.

The Importance of the Blessing

In Genesis there are numerous examples of the importance of the father's blessing. This blessing was so important that Jacob was willing to deceive Isaac into giving it to him instead of Esau to whom it rightfully belonged. In Genesis 31 is the example of Jacob unknowingly speaking a curse over Rachel. As Jacob, his wives and children leave Mesopotamia, Rachel secretly takes household gods with her. Laban sets out to retrieve the idols. As Jacob is confronted by Laban, he challenges Laban to search all their belongings for the idols and then adds the curse, "If you find anyone who has your gods, he shall not live" (Genesis 31:32). Laban did not find the idols but shortly after this Rachel died in childbirth.

With authority comes the power to bless or curse and we must recognize in our words blessing or cursing. In frustration a husband blurts out to his wife, "You'll never learn to keep house", a father to a son, "You are so clumsy. You'll never be coordinated"; a mother to a daughter, "Shame on you". Most of these curses are words carelessly spoken, inflamed by anger, frustration, jealousy, defensiveness, revenge, etc. In the midst of these situations we have an enemy stirring up the pot, encouraging us to speak curses instead of blessings.

We can also impose curses on persons outside our authority, to friends and acquaintances and even to people we don't know at all. With our words we also invoke curses on ourselves. Have you ever spoken or thought the following or perhaps something similar?

I'd rather die than _____.

I never have enough money to go around. It's always been that way in my family.

Nothing good ever happens to me.

It's driving me crazy.

I'll never _____ again.

God will not protect us from ourselves for that would violate our free will. He will, however, work within to convict us of what we have done. It is then up to us to right the situation. To correct a self-imposed curse we must first repent of speaking the curse. Next we must cancel the curse and finally give a right confession. For an example let's look at the second statement, "I never have enough money to go around. It's always been that way in my family." First we must confess and repent of having said this statement, acknowledging that it is not according to God's Word and asking forgiveness for having said it. Next we cancel the statement, "In the name of Jesus I break the curse of this statement over myself and my family." And finally we make the positive confession, "I affirm in my life, Lord, that you are the provider of all I have need of (2 Corinthians 9:8) and that you will not withhold any good thing from me (Psalm 84:11)."

From Generation to Generation

Blessings and curses can also be generational in nature. Our obedience will bless those to come. One of the greatest blessings in the Bible was given to Abraham.

I will surely bless you and make your descendants as numerous as the stars in the sky and as the sand on the seashore. Your descendants will take possession of the cities of their enemies, and through your offspring all nations on earth will be blessed, because you have obeyed me. Genesis 22:17-18

We are heirs to this blessing, but God's blessings are always conditional on our obedience.

Know therefore that the Lord your God is God; he is the faithful God, keeping his covenant of love to a thousand generations of those who love him and keep his commands. Deuteronomy 7:9

Curses are also passed on from generation to generation.

You shall not make for yourself an idol in the form of anything in heaven above or on the earth beneath or in the waters below. You shall not bow down to them or worship them; for I, the Lord your God, am a jealous God, punishing the children for the sin of the fathers to the third and fourth generations of those who hate me, but showing love to a thousand generations of those who love me and keep my commandments. Exodus 20:4-6

Cursing and Blessing of Physical Objects

In addition to words, physical objects may also be vehicles for blessings and curses. Two objects for blessing are anointing oil and the emblems used in the Lord's supper, the bread and wine. The blessings conveyed in this manner are not inherent in the object themselves. It is only by faith and obedience that the blessing is invoked.

Physical objects can be used in limitless ways for curses. From the above quote from Exodus 20 it can be seen that physical objects connected with occult (idolatry) are the vehicle for curses. Statues, jewelry, symbols, literature, etc., come under this category. Numerous objects are unknowingly brought into homes thereby placing the homes and occupants under a curse. As with any sin, ignorance is no excuse. We need to be knowledgeable concerning the occult to avoid bringing curses on ourselves and our families.

On one occasion I was praying with a lady from Okinawa who was having a very difficult time sleeping. She would wake up in the middle of the night sensing that something was in the room with her. She could not rest well and was exhausted. In the course of our conversation I learned that she was a fairly new believer and that all of her family were still living in Okinawa and were devout Buddhists. She shared how unhappy they were that she had become a Christian. As we talked she told me how her mother would send her objects that she knew had been cursed in a ceremony commonly practiced by Buddhists. As we were praying I saw in my mind a picture of a dragon and asked her if she had anything with a picture of a dragon on it. She said her mother gave her as a gift a beautiful set of silk pajamas that had a very ornate dragon embroidered on the front. Also, that she wore them to bed every night. I told her perhaps she should not sleep in them but rather take them out and burn them. She came back the next week, and told me that after she burned the pajamas she had no more trouble sleeping!

God's protection from curses is available within a limited sphere. "Like a fluttering sparrow or a darting swallow, an undeserved curse does not come to rest" (Proverbs 26:2). A curse cannot be effective unless there is a cause, namely sin. God cannot protect us from cursing ourselves. Nor is protection necessarily available from curses sent to us by others if we are harboring sin in our lives. On the other hand, I have discovered that there are times when curses come my way that do affect me and I am not harboring any sin that I am aware of.

Where the Battle Begins

The very first thing we must do in spiritual warfare is acknowledge that it does exist and that we have enemies in the spiritual realm.

The actual engagement in battle comes with the act of submitting ourselves to God and being obedient to His direction.

> But he gives us more grace. That is why Scripture says: "God opposes the proud but gives grace to the humble." Submit yourselves, then, to God. Resist the devil, and he will flee from you. James 4:6-7

This passage first gives us the warning that God opposes the proud. Pride exalts itself above God and wants its own power. Therefore, it is the enemy of the directive in this passage that we submit to God. Pride was the downfall of Lucifer and Adam and Eve. Arrogantly thinking that this will not be our downfall is dangerous. If Lucifer, Adam and Eve succumbed to this, we can too. Jeremiah 49:16 says, "the pride of your heart has deceived you."

Submission involves giving up control of our lives and trusting God to take care of us.

The majority of us have learned to be in control of our lives and we feel comfortable there. Being out-of-control can be very uncomfortable and frightening until we make the choice to trust God with our lives.

Control is a false belief (unbiblical) and is self-centered. It is a tactic of Satan who wants us to believe we are better off with self in control than allowing God to be in control. This is pride in action.

James also says that God gives grace to the humble. Only the humble person can truly submit himself to God and allow Him to be in control.

As we humble ourselves in submission and then resist Satan, the result will be that he will flee. This then is the beginning of warfare. Without submission and obedience to God the battle is lost.[9]

Warfare with the Past

As Christians, until we come to the point of involving ourselves in our own spiritual warfare we are very vulnerable. Satan can easily take advantage of us. The Bible often contrasts darkness and light, the darkness being areas where Satan has legal access and the light being God. As we become aware of spiritual warfare we need to look at our past to find those areas of darkness where Satan already has legal access and get rid of these strongholds.

There are three ways in which these areas of darkness are created within us.

1. It comes through generational sin. As has been discussed under Blessings and Cursings these strongholds are passed from one generation to the next. In the immaturity of childhood we are understandably ill equipped to recognize spiritual warfare. Therefore, unless our parents are knowledgeable in this area and break these generational strongholds, we inherit them until we mature to the point of being able to get rid of them ourselves.

2. It comes through wounding inflicted by others in childhood or adulthood by means of sexual, physical, psychological and spiritual abuse. As children we may have no recourse when abuse occurs. Even as adults unless we are rooted and grounded in God and are knowledgeable we may believe we have no choice but to accept the abuse. God's Truth is that we do have a choice. We do not have to accept abuse into our inner being.

3. It comes through willful, sinful actions in childhood or adulthood. The consequences of sin come about whether or not we are knowledgeable concerning that sin. Persistent sin results in strongholds of darkness. We are responsible for making the choices to allow these in our lives.[10]

If we have survived childhood and youth into adulthood the chances of us having enemy strongholds in our lives are overwhelming. Few Christians recognize or want to accept the fact of these strongholds in their lives. We have thought in terms of the dramatic manifestation of demonic possession as depicted in movies and books. While possession is impossible for the Christian, demonization (a stronghold) is not. Demonization is far more subtle and deceptive. Satan does not want us to know he's there. Of the Christians who acknowledge the possibility of demonization few understand how easy it is for these strongholds to have legal rights in their lives. It is as easy as making a choice. For with that persistent choice comes God's presence or the enemy's darkness.

All of these dark areas keep us from being the whole person God intended us to be. We will have little victory in our lives when we are warring on two fronts, within and without. God wants to replace darkness with the light of His being. Only as these strongholds are removed will we have a closer and closer relationship with God. The whole point of spiritual warfare is to make choices that produce God's light within instead of darkness. Therefore, it is extremely important for us to go back and deal with the past. For further insights see both the Inner Healing and Deliverance sections of this manual.

The Weapons of Your Warfare

Our battles with Satan can be likened to earthly warfare. The tactics are similar. However, earthly weapons would have no effect in the spiritual realm s God has given us spiritual weapons. "The weapons we fight with are not the weapons of the world. On the contrary, they have divine power to demolish strongholds" (2 Corinthians 10:4). Just as soldiers learn to use their earthly weapons, so we, as Christians, must learn to use our spiritual weapons. Learning to use your weapons is a process and takes time and practice. You won't be fully trained overnight. Learn by doing and keep practicing!

I. A Clean Heart

This is your most important defense weapon and maintenance tool for other weapons. "We should realize that the greatest defense we can have against the devil is to maintain an honest heart before God.[11]

> *Create in me a pure heart, O God, and renew a steadfast spirit within me. Do not cast me from your presence or take your Holy Spirit from me. Psalm 51:10-11*

The psalmist knew that a clean heart is absolutely essential for an unobstructed relationship with the Lord. Sin breaks the relationship. Persistence in sin weakens our weapons and creates an area of darkness within us to which Satan has legal access. We are warned in 2 Corinthians 2:10-11 to not let Satan take advantage of us in this way.

Repentance and forgiveness (both receiving and granting) are the things that maintain a clean heart. "Be kind and compassionate to one another, forgiving each other, just as in Christ God forgave you" (Ephesians 4:32). Notice that this is a command. It is not an option.. Neither does it depend on anything else in our circumstances such as our emotions. There is no waiting for the right time. The time is always now for repentance and forgiveness. Sin and unforgiveness are both conscious and unconscious. We are responsible for dealing with what is conscious. God is the one who reveals unconscious sin to us. We are then responsible for it.

Defensiveness is something we can easily fall into in the area of maintaining a clean heart. At its root is pride and God opposes the proud. "When the Holy Spirit shows us an area that needs repentance, we must overcome the instinct to defend ourselves. . . . For you to succeed in warfare, your self-preservation instincts must be submitted to the Lord Jesus"[12] Aaron is a prime example of defending ourselves when confronted with our sin (Exodus 32:1-6; 21-24). When Moses was gone on Mt. Sinai for forty days the people came to Aaron and asked him to make an idol. He readily agreed, not putting up any protest and made the golden calf himself. But when Moses confronted Aaron he blamed the people and said, "Then they gave me the gold, and I threw it into the fire, and out came this calf!" (Exodus 32:24). This sounds like a defense given by a child. What parent would believe this story? God and Moses certainly didn't. Whether we use a naive defense such as Aaron's or a more sophisticated one, the result is the same. We don't fool God and we perpetuate the broken relationship with Him. Better to confess our sin immediately when confronted and mend our relationship with the Lord.

A dirty heart causes our armor to be out of alignment.

II. Discernment

Discernment is a vital tool in warfare.

We have three voices going through our heads: our own, God's and Satan's. Therefore, we must learn to discern which is which.

Webster defines "discern" as "to separate a thing mentally from another or others; recognize as separate or different ... to perceive or recognize; make out clearly"

The man without the Spirit does not accept the things that come from the Spirit of God, for they are foolishness to him, and he cannot understand them, because they are spiritually discerned. 1 Corinthians 2:14

The ability to discern is given to us by the Holy Spirit when we become believers. As with many of the weapons <u>it develops with use</u>. "But solid food is for the mature who by constant use have trained themselves to distinguish good from evil" (Hebrews 5:14). God should be our only source of discernment. He is the one who wants to direct, guide and inform us. We are commanded in Exodus 20:3 to have no other gods before Him.

There are two major areas in which we need discernment if we are to be successful in warfare. In both cases the discernment is from the Holy Spirit.

The first is the discernment of God's Truth. The Spirit reveals to us how the Word applies to us in any given place or time. The same scripture may be used at different times in our lives with different applications to our circumstances. Discernment is for this moment.

The second area is that of God's direction, guidance and information for us personally aside from the Word. Normally God communicates directly to our minds through thought but it can also be through mental pictures, visions and dreams. He also uses the words of other people to confirm something He has said to us.

Here are some important points in using discernment:

1. Discernment will come only when we truly believe that God wants to communicate with us. John 10 likens this communication to sheep and their shepherd. ". . . his sheep follow him because they know his voice. But they will never follow a stranger; in fact, they will run away from him because they do not recognize a stranger's voice" verses 4,5). "My sheep listen to my voice; I know them, and they follow me" (verse 27). God not only talks in a voice we can hear but He expects us to learn to know His voice.

2. Discernment comes with the choice to listen. We can turn God off if we choose to do so. We usually make this choice when we don't like what God is saying to us or don't want to be obedient.

3. Discernment should always be sought from God and never from the enemy. God's Word should always be our reference book. It is our plumb line. He will never tell us anything contrary to His written word.

4. Discernment comes with practice. Just as we learn to recognize someone's voice on the telephone before they identify themselves so we learn to identify God's voice.

    1 Samuel 3:1-10 gives us an example of hearing the Lord for the first time. God called Samuel by name but he did not recognize it and thought it was the priest Eli. When Samuel went to Eli he was told Eli was not the one calling Samuel. This happened three times. Eli finally discerned that it was God and told Samuel when it happened again to answer God.

God speaks to us in a variety of ways just as we speak in a variety of ways. At times it will be obvious and at others it will be a whisper that you almost miss.

5. Ask God for confirmation of what He is communicating to you. We are human and make mistakes. Therefore, it is wise to make sure of what God is saying. The confirmation may come very quickly or may take time. Wait for God so that you do not get ahead of Him.

Discernment is closely tied to all other weapons of warfare, but especially to a clean heart.

III. God's Armor

God's armor is a gift from Him at the time of our salvation. It is His perfect defense and offense for us to use against the enemy. It is nothing less than Jesus Christ Himself in all His perfection. Your armor is (Ephesians 6:13-17):

- The belt of truth. In John 14:6 Jesus says, "I am the way and the truth and the life."

- The breastplate of righteousness. "The Lord our righteousness" (Jeremiah 23:6).

- The shoes of the gospel of peace. "For he himself is our peace" (Ephesians 2:14)

- The shield of faith. ". . .Jesus, the author and perfecter of our faith . . ." (Hebrews 12:2)

- The helmet of salvation. "salvation is found in no one else . . ." (Acts 4:12).

- The sword of the Spirit, which is the Word of God. "In the beginning was the Word, and the Word was with God, and the Word was God. He was with God in the beginning" (John 1:1-2).

Let's take a closer look at these pieces of armor as related to our spiritual warfare:

- The belt of truth holds all the other armor in place. Without the belt of Truth other pieces can slip out of place. Since our personal warfare is in the mind this is where the Truth must be applied and believed. When the enemy gives us any thought that is not consistent with God's Word we reject it. We must so saturate ourselves with the Truth that we can have it at our fingertips and quickly make choices between God's Truth and the enemy's lies.

- The breastplate of righteousness gives us an eternal standing before God. We are clothed in Jesus' robe of righteousness and although we know this in the spiritual realm the reality in the physical realm is that we sin. With that sin our breastplate slips out of alignment making us vulnerable to the enemy. To put this piece of armor back in alignment we must use confession and repentance. Daily victory in the arena of spiritual warfare is at stake.

- The shoes of the gospel of peace give us the personal peace of the Prince of Peace Himself. They also give us corporate peace if we allow it to rule our hearts. Soldiers are given peacekeeping duties as well as warfare duties. Reconciliation is part of our job description as Christians. However if we allow resentment and bitterness to rule our hearts the peace will not be there.

- The shield of faith is our defense against everything the enemy would fling at our minds: the lies, accusations, temptations and half-truths. We must be in sync with the shield of faith for it to be effective. We do this by allowing our knowledge of God and His Word to increase in our lives thereby building our faith (belief) in God.

- The helmet of salvation is your eternal possession. It will not come off with victories or losses in the battles of life. It is the assurance that no matter how you are doing in Satan's realm you have the ultimate victory in the eternal realm. It protects our minds where the war rages.

- The sword of the Spirit is an offensive as well as defensive weapon. The more we know of God's Word the better we can wield the sword. (The sword of the Spirit has also been addressed in a separate section because of its importance. See page 7-20.)

Jesus is the only one who wore His armor perfectly. It never slipped out of place. Our armor is Christ in all His perfection but it can slip out of place when we sin. We must understand what each piece of armor is made of, how it functions and how we keep it in alignment.

Look in God's mirror daily, making adjustments as needed.[13]

IV. Authority

Understanding our authority starts by understanding our position in Christ. Authority, in this context, is given only to those who belong to the right family, God's family.

Paul uses adoption as an illustration of our relationship with God after salvation. We get a new birth certificate with God listed as our father and we are now heirs and co-heirs with Christ. As a member of God's family we are in a position to be given authority. It is delegated authority. Jesus said, "... All authority in heaven and on Earth has been given to me" (Matthew 28:18). He in turn delegates that authority to us. We are a representative of the highest authority, God Himself. The analogy of a policeman is often used to help understand this concept. A policeman has no authority or power of his own. The police chief has given the policeman authority and power to dispense law and order on his behalf. The badge and identification the policeman carries show everyone he has this delegated authority. It is the same with believers. All creatures in the spiritual realm know we Christians have delegated authority. Perhaps our badge, in the spiritual realm, is the seal of the Holy Spirit. All believers, whether new or of long-standing, have the same authority. How well it is used depends on how much experience has been gained in the use of authority and the wisdom acquired concerning its use.

> *Obey your leaders and submit to their authority. They keep watch over you as men who must give an account. Obey them so that their work will be a joy, not a burden, for that would be of no advantage to you. Hebrews 13:17*

Along with learning to use authority we must also learn to stay under authority. You must stay under the spiritual authority of those over you, whether it be husband, father or pastor. And don't forget our ultimate authority, God. Stay under the protective shadow of His wings. To move out from under spiritual authority is opening the door for Satan.

V. The Power of the Holy Spirit

It takes more than authority to carry out what you are commanded to do. Power is needed to back up that authority. Believers have the power of the Holy Spirit. As with authority we have no power of our own. Paul makes it clear that this power is God's, not ours.

> *But we have this treasure in jars of clay to show that this all-surpassing power is from God and not from us. 2 Corinthians 4:7*

The Holy Spirit's power is the power behind all our weapons, whether defensive or offensive. It is protective in the sense that it strengthens us in all areas of our lives so that we can better fight the enemy. ". . .being strengthened with all power according to his glorious might so that you may have great endurance and patience. . ." (Colossians 1:11). It is the power we need to move from Satan's side to God's side, to become more Christlike. It is the power that sends the enemy retreating in our lives.

When Jesus was on Earth, His source of power was the Holy Spirit. He did not use any power of His own and was obedient to the Father. Jesus told His disciples that they would do the works He did and even greater ones because He was sending the same power source to them (John 14:12). We have that same power source and can use it in the same way Jesus did. Jesus was tempted on a personal level by Satan in the wilderness and defeated him by the use of the Holy Spirit's power only. Unlike us, Jesus had the power of His own to defeat Satan but He didn't use it. He was being our example, showing what we can do with that same power. The Holy Spirit was also Jesus' source of power in ministry and He tells us we can do those same works. Ministry, although publicly seen, is a very personal matter. Success in ministry begins with success in personal warfare.

Power is dependent upon all the other weapons already mentioned: a clean heart, discernment, the alignment of your armor and authority. Authority and power go hand in hand. Without authority, power is not available. Without power, there is nothing to back up authority. Without a clean heart, clear discernment and armor in alignment, power and authority are greatly diminished.

When using authority and power we must stay under God's authority and direction. Doing things in the flesh leaves us vulnerable to Satan. Pride undermines power. It is not our power but the Holy Spirit's. We must use it humbly and wisely.

VI. The Blood of Jesus

The Blood is both an offensive and defensive weapon as well as being a maintenance tool for other weapons.

In the Old Testament God pointed to the cleansing property the Blood would have when He outlines its use when sprinkled on the altar as a sign of the covenant between God and His people and as atonement for the people's sin. Jesus fulfilled all the requirements of the Old Covenant. We no longer have to offer sacrifices because Jesus did it for us once and for all. Although the Blood of Jesus was seen in the physical realm only at the crucifixion, its existence is still very real in the spiritual realm.

> *For you know that it was not with perishable things such as silver or gold that you were redeemed from the empty way of life handed down to you from your forefathers, but with the precious blood of Christ, a lamb without blemish or defect. 1 Peter 1:18-19*

Notice that in this verse Peter is telling us the opposite of what our minds would logically tell us. We think of gold and silver as imperishable and blood as perishable, but the opposite is true. The reality is the Blood exists and is imperishable in the spiritual realm. It is the cleansing agent that gives us a clean heart thereby giving us clear discernment and aligned armor as well as power and authority.

The blood also protects and can be used to cleanse areas of demons as well. This is based upon the fact that Satan cannot penetrate the Blood. Where the Blood is applied, Satan cannot go. (Exodus 12:12,13) The cleansing property as applied to ourselves personally is automatic when we seek forgiveness or forgive. However, in the case of protection and clearing areas of demonic activity it must be specifically applied and claimed.

VI. The Name of Jesus

> *Therefore God exalted him to the highest place and gave him the name that is above every name, that at the name of Jesus every knee should bow, in heaven and on earth and under the earth, and every tongue confess that Jesus Christ is Lord . . .Philippians 2:9-11*

As adopted children now belonging to God's family we have the authority to use Jesus' name in what we are assigned to do. Jesus' name is the key to unlocking power.

> *And whatever you do, whether in word or deed, do it all in the name of the Lord Jesus, giving thanks to God the Father through him. Colossians 3:17*

Just as with authority and power, there is a responsibility that goes with using Jesus' name. His name encompasses everything that Jesus is. Whatever we do in His name must be consistent with His character. We cannot lie, murder, steal, etc. in His name. Using Jesus' name must be done in His character and His will.

How do we know His character and His will? "If you remain in me and my words remain in you, ask whatever you wish, and it will be given you" (John 15:7). The "ask whatever you wish" is qualified with "if you abide in me and my words abide in you". Is there a person in your life that you know so well that you can predict what they will do in any given situation? So well, that you know what gift they would or would not appreciate. Think about the business representative who knows his boss so well that he can conduct business on his behalf, confidently knowing what the boss would or would not approve of. In our relationship with the Lord we should know Him better than any other person in our lives and be able to act on His behalf and in His will.

VII. Binding and Loosing

Matthew 16:19 and 18:18 state ". . . whatever you bind on earth will be bound in heaven and whatever you loose on earth will be loosed in heaven". Here we are given authority to "bind" and to "loose". In more familiar terms we could use the words "forbid" and "permit".

Binding is the limiting of activity and power which we have authority to do in the Name of Jesus .

Loosing is permitting or even inviting. It is loosing the things of God to operate in a situation. God's purposes are carried out by asking in prayer for His will to be done.

Binding and loosing work together. The strategy is to forbid the enemy to continue working in a situation and then release the things of God to go to work in the same situation and turn it around. This is an example of the authority given us by Jesus when He says, *"I have given you authority to trample on snakes and scorpions and to overcome all the power of the enemy; nothing will harm you"* (Luke 10:19).

Binding and loosing can be used both offensively and defensively. Offensively it is used as protection against what the enemy could do in our lives. The following prayer pattern is an example of using binding and loosing for protection.

A Binding Prayer for Protection

> In the name of Jesus Christ and by the power of His Cross and Blood I bind the satanic spirits, powers, and forces of the earth, the air, the water, the fire, the netherworld and the satanic forces of nature. I rebuke any curses, hexes, or spells and send them back to where they came from. I claim the protection of the shed Blood of Jesus Christ over (name things you want protected: ourselves, others, things, home, car, etc) [14]

The following is an example of using binding and loosing. An incident in our lives brings on overwhelming fear. We recognize that this is not what God wants in our lives (2 Timothy 1:7). We also know that God wants us to trust Him and rest in His peace (John 14:27). We have made the choice to fear. It is therefore up to us to make the choice to rid ourselves of that spirit. We can say to the spirit of fear, "I forbid you to operate further in my life in the Name of Jesus". We then release God to work by saying, "In the Name of Jesus I invite the Holy Spirit to fill me with His peace. Release within me trust of you, Lord, and change my will to resist and conquer the spirit of fear." This is how we personally use binding and loosing. Remember that fear can also be an emotion and may not be gone instantly. We have bound up the enemy from working further but we also must choose not to give in to the emotion of fear. Fear can breed further fear. Emotions do subside but it may not be immediately.

Until we are comfortable binding and loosing, prayer patterns may be helpful, but beware of using them as a magic formula. Binding and loosing can be done just as powerfully in your own words. Of course, there is no greater example of meeting the enemy head-on than Jesus during His temptation in the wilderness. The Word is mighty.

As has been discussed earlier in the Authority and Power sections, discernment and wisdom must be used with our weapons. Binding and loosing should not be used indiscriminately.

VIII. The Sword of the Spirit

". . . which is the word of God" (Ephesians 6:17).

The Word is both defensive and offensive. In its defensive stance the Word is both for ourselves and the enemy. The reason many of us are defeated by Satan is that we do not abide in the Word. John praised the young men of the early church by saying, "I write to you, young men, because you are strong; and the word of God lives in you, and you have overcome the evil one" (1 John 2:14). These young men were victors in the spiritual realm because God's word lived in them. How does God's Word live in us?

> *For the word of God is living and active. Sharper than any double-edged sword, it penetrates even to dividing soul and spirit, joints and marrow; it judges the thoughts and attitudes of the heart Hebrews 4:12*

The Word shows us what needs to be removed from our lives and what the replacement is to be. If we are to live the Word, not merely profess it, we must let the Word change our very being. "Victory begins with the name of Jesus on your lips; but it will not be consummated until the nature of Jesus is in your heart"[15]. The more Christlike we are in nature the less Satan has to attack.

When Satan goes on the attack we have God's Word to defend us. The ultimate illustration is Jesus' temptation in the wilderness. As Satan presents each temptation, Jesus counters with the Word and Satan is left with no response.

Our stance in spiritual warfare should not only be defensive but offensive as well. The Sword of the Spirit can be used as an aggressive weapon. In Matthew 12:29 Jesus states, "... how can anyone enter a strong man's house and carry off his possessions unless he first ties up the strong man? Then he can rob his house". We can so war against Satan that we tie him up and take away what he claims is his.

Behind the Sword of the Spirit is the Holy Spirit. We pick up the Sword and put it in the Spirit's hand but He is the one who wields it. We must be in submission to the Holy Spirit for it to be effective. If we are trusting in the wrong sword or the wrong strength we are essentially tying the Spirit's hands in using the Sword.

IX. Prayer

Many volumes have been written on prayer. The intent here is not to explore prayer completely but to relate its importance as a weapon in spiritual warfare. Every prayer is spiritual warfare.

From a spiritual warfare perspective our goal is to help establish God's kingdom and will both in our own lives and in every aspect of this fallen world. In doing this we are pushing back Satan's territory, making it smaller and smaller. Everything that God has directed us to pray for works towards this end.

In this prayer from Matthew 6:9-13 Jesus is giving a model for what is important in prayer.

""**Our Father in heaven, hallowed be your name.**" Hallowed means respected or revered. What He did to make it possible for us to call Him our Father is all one needs to see to begin to become a true worshiper. Praise and worship are the primary activities of heaven. And so it is to be for the believer here on earth. Worship is our number one priority in ministry. The more we live as citizens of heaven, the more heaven's activities infect our lifestyles. Prayer is our opportunity to minister to God. Do you realize what he gave for you to call him Papa, God? God is completely separate from everything that is dark, everything that is evil. God so fills all of heaven there is nothing hidden there. Derek Prince, "If you only have ten minutes to pray take about eight of them to worship God, it's amazing what you can ask for in two minutes." Worship is a privilege to minister unto God. We've been called to minister unto the Lord because we have been privileged to minister unto the Lord. He gives us free access to come before Him.

"**Thy kingdom come, thy will be done on earth as it is in heaven.**" This is the primary focus for all prayer-if it exists in heaven, it is to be loosed on earth. It's the praying Christian who looses heaven's expression here. When the believer prays according to the revealed will of God, faith is specific and focused. Faith grabs hold of that reality. Enduring faith doesn't let go. Everything about your prayer life is to bring the reality of that world into this one. Jesus here encapsulates one purpose of prayer-to minister to Him and to bring His reality down, to anchor our lives into where we are going when we die and to bring that reality into this one. The will of God is seen in the ruling presence of God, for "Where the Spirit of the Lord is, there is liberty." When the King of kings manifest His dominion, the fruit of that dominion is liberty. That is the realm called the Kingdom of God. Heaven is the model, it is the real, the world with substance. This is the inferior realm. It's saying, "God we depend on your rulership being seen in the circumstances that we're confronting. We are dependent on your lordship being demonstrated in this disease, in this home, this business, school. Bring the reality of your world into this one." It is a violent apprehending. Faith is active, it's not a passive thing. By nature it is enduring, doesn't let go until it gets what it is after.

"**Give us this day our daily bread...**" Heaven sets the standard for a Christian's material world-enough to satisfy the desires born of God and enough "for every good work." "And my God shall supply all your needs according to His riches in glory by Christ Jesus.(Phil. 4:19). Heaven's resources are to affect us here and now. Use heavens bounty as the standard for your cupboard. That's what he's telling us to pray. Jesus is illustrating how it is in heaven. This is how a kingdom life is focused. He summarizes this all in vs. 33. Seek First...."and all this other stuff that concerns you will be added to you."

"**Forgive us our debts as we forgive our debtors.**" Are there people in heaven holding onto bitterness? Is there any unforgiveness in heaven, obviously not. Heaven provides the model for our relationships here on earth. He is illustrating the reality of heaven in how it affects our relationships and attitudes toward people. Think about this, this is the model for prayer and we are to pray without ceasing. If this is the model for prayer and I must pray without ceasing then I must arm myself with a continual commitment to not be offended. It's praying, - I want heaven to influence everything in my life.

"And lead us not into temptation," There is no temptation or sin in heaven. Neither is there any presence of evil. Keeping separate from evil is practical evidence of our coming under our King's rule. This prayer does not imply that God wants to tempt us. We know from James 1:13 that it is impossible for God to entice us to sin. "When tempted, no one should say, "God is tempting me." For God cannot be tempted by evil, nor does he tempt anyone" We pray this because it's good for you and me to recognize our vulnerabilities and to face our need for grace. It's saying to God, I realize I am made of the same stuff as anybody else and apart from your grace I am as capable of any sin as anybody is on the planet. The person who realizes that has put a prayer guard over their blind spot. The person who realizes that has just established angelic presence to watch over the blind spot. This prayer is actually a request for God not to promote us beyond what our character can handle. Sometimes our anointing and gift are ready for increase of responsibility, but our character isn't.

"Deliver us from the evil one..." A heart modeled after heaven has great success in spiritual warfare. "Submit to God. Resist the devil and he will flee from you." James 4:7. The believer is to be completely free from all-satanic influence and attachments. Within the surrendered heart is the potential prayer to forever change a neighbor's life. We are buffeted by cute prayer sayings and still much of the church remains prayerless. It's not the busyness of schedule that keeps people from prayer; it's the busyness of heart. It's the need for constant stimulation from the outside; noise, activity. Sometimes Christians are guilty of staying busy to keep themselves from being sensitive to what God really is saying and wanting to do.

"Yours is the kingdom and power and glory." The kingdom of God is His possession, which is why He alone can give it to us. All through the Scriptures we hear the declarations of praise similar to this one contained in His model prayer declaring that all glory and power belong to Him."[16]

Once again, this prayer has two main objectives: (1) Minister to God out of an intimate personal relationship; and (2) bring the reality of His rulership (the Kingdom) to earth.

X. A Mighty Weapon - Praise

> *But you are a chosen people, a royal priesthood, a holy nation, a people belonging to God, that you may declare the praises of him who called you out of darkness into his wonderful light. 1 Peter 2:9*

Throughout Scripture, God initiates agreements (covenants) with His people. In Psalm 81 God puts forth praise as a covenant. God says, "if you will, then I will." Psalm 81 starts out by describing and commanding praise on our part and then goes on to give the reasons we are to do this.[17]

First, we are to praise God because He commands it. Verse 4 states, "This is a decree for Israel, an ordinance of the God of Jacob." It is not an option. This takes an act of our will to be obedient to praise no matter what else is going on in our lives. Our refusal to praise God is rebellion against Him.

Praising God is a witness to others. "He established it as a statute for Joseph" (verse 5). Praise always points to the one being praised. It is God-centered, telling of who He is and what He does.

We also praise God because He has delivered us from the bondage of sin. "I removed the burden from their shoulders; their hands were set free from the basket" (verse 6). This verse obviously refers to God freeing the Israelites from Egyptian slavery. But God is still in the business of delivering us from slavery, slavery to sin, demonic strongholds and "religion" (having a form of godliness but denying its power, 2 Timothy 3:5).

"In your distress you called and I rescued you, I answered you out of a thundercloud;" (verse 7). We are to praise God because He answers our prayers. We should never lose our sense of awe at the fact that God listens to our cries and answers. Not only does He answer but He gives us what is best for us in His will, not what we deserve.

Finally, we are to praise God because He tests us. "I tested you at the waters of Meribah" (verse 7). In the midst of trials, temptations and tests we praise God for these and for what they do in our lives to mold us into the image of Christ.

> *Praise the Lord. Praise the Lord from the heavens, praise him in the heights above. Praise him, all his angels, praise him, all his heavenly hosts. Praise him, sun and moon, praise him, all you shining stars. Praise him, you highest heavens and you waters above the skies. Let them praise the name of the Lord, for he commanded and they were created. He set them in place for ever and ever; he gave a decree that will never pass away. Praise the Lord from the earth, you great sea creatures and all ocean depths, lightning and hail, snow and clouds, stormy winds that do his bidding, you mountains and all hills, fruit trees and all cedars, wild animals and all cattle, small creatures and flying birds, kings of the earth and all nations, you princes and all rulers on earth, young men and maidens, old men and children. Let them praise the name of the Lord, for his name alone is exalted; his splendor is above the earth and the heavens. He has raised up for his people a horn, the praise of all his saints, of Israel, the people close to his heart. Praise the Lord. Psalm 148*

Battle in Ministry

If we are ineffective Christians, sitting back and letting others do God's work, Satan has us right where he wants us. When we are at the center of God's will we are a threat to Satan and what is a threat to him he attacks. There are some principles of ministry we need to follow in order not to get out from under God's protection.

First, we must walk in humility at all times. Without humility we are not submitted to God to use as He chooses.

Second, we must minister in truth and light.

> *"How can you say to your brother, `Brother, let me take the speck out of your eye', when you yourself fail to see the plank in your own eye? You hypocrite, first take the plank out of your eye, and then you will see clearly to remove the speck from your brother's eye." Luke 6:42*

God uses the areas of our life that are in His light to minister to others. The areas where we are still walking in darkness should not be used to minister to others. If we try to use these areas we will only be perpetuating the enemy's darkness in others. We must be very aware of the shortcomings in our own lives, those areas that still need God's cleansing and healing. It takes humility to back away from these areas in ministry and allow someone else who is walking in light to do the ministering.

Third, we cannot take the burden of ministry on ourselves.

> *"Come to me, all you who are weary and burdened, and I will give you rest. Take my yoke upon you and learn from me, for I am gentle and humble in heart, and you will find rest for your souls. For my yoke is easy and my burden is light." Matthew 11:28-30*

We need to constantly be on watch for burdens we have taken on ourselves, and for work we are doing in the flesh. This leads to burnout. When we find ourselves in this position Jesus bids us come to Him for rest. The burdens are His to begin with. When we allow Him to shoulder the burdens, our part is light work and we will be able to go the distance.

Part of releasing all burdens to God is being able to trust Him completely for all our needs. If we do not trust we carry the burden. It is arrogance on our part to think that we can do a better job than God. He is well able to meet every need, physically, mentally and spiritually. We cannot use excuses that we are not equipped or worthy. First Corinthians 1:27- 28 tells us who God chooses to use.

In a sermon based on this scripture, Michael Evans said, "We have five categories: the foolish, the weak, the lowly, the despised and the nobodies. (This is the way we are seen by most of the world). Now we are in this army and the fools are the front lines, the weak are the second. Perhaps you've been thinking you were too weak for proclaiming and demonstrating the message of the Cross? WRONG! You're perfect for this army. Step up right behind the fools who are such fools they are not ashamed to be in the front! If you are not good enough for the second row fall in with the lowly, despised and the nobodies. Is this crazy or what!"[18] What a motley army God calls together. Having it altogether is not a qualification in God's kingdom. In fact, it can be a disqualification.

Fourth, be prepared for God's training. Be ready to submit and be obedient in those times when God puts us through tough survival courses. During these times it is easy to blame everything on the enemy. Our nature wants to believe that God would only bring us good things, which He does. But, beware of putting your own definition on what God's good is. He allows these rough times to smooth our rough edges, to refine us in His fire so that we become usable vessels in His service. We need to develop a positive and thankful attitude to this refining and training. When we do we will also have the end result in view as we go the course.

Fifth, when we minister we will be under someone's authority and we need to stay under that authority. Lines of authority are God's system and He is the ultimate authority. As such, if we get out of line, we are also out of line with God and therefore, outside His protection. Do we have to always agree with our authority figures? No, but rebellion is never correct. It is sin. We may come to a place where we must choose to obey God rather than men but we should never develop the attitude of rebellion. Daniel is a good example of this position. He disagreed at times with the kings over him but never developed the attitude of rebellion toward them. As with Daniel prayer is always in order in this position.

For more information on this topic see page N-1, Spiritual Warfare and Healing.

Maturity In Battle

Maturity is the ability to make right choices at a critical time. All that we have talked about influences our maturity in battle. Do we live in truth and light, knowing where the battle is and who is involved in it? Do we know the Scriptures? Do we have an intimate relationship with God? Do we know the enemy? Are we familiar with the consequences of the choices we make? Is our heart pure and bent toward obedience? Do we know how to use the weapons at our disposal? Each one of these questions answered in the affirmative contributes to our maturity and therefore our ability to make right choices.

Our position in the Body is to minister and receive ministry so that each one of us reaches maturity and Christlikeness which is the victory in personal spiritual warfare. As a participating member in the Body our spiritual warfare goal is corporate. Paul concludes Romans 12 by saying, "Do not be overcome by evil but overcome evil with good." None of us can take on the kingdom of darkness alone. Paul, in the context of the Body, is telling us to be overcomers. Christ expects His body to overcome the kingdom of darkness, together.

> *To him who overcomes, I will give the right to sit with me on my throne, just as I overcame and sat down with my Father on his throne. Revelation 3:21*

Only when this is done will the Body be His pure, spotless Bride who is ready to co-rule with Him for eternity.[19]

Section 8: Ministry Organization

The Purpose and Mission

Wholeness Ministries originated as a result of God revealing to many people the need to train and equip people to function as "prayer ministers" - to minister to those in need of physical, spiritual, mental or emotional healing throughout the church and the community. Wholeness Ministries provides a safe place where ministry can occur with well trained prayer ministers in a private, confidential setting, as well as a place where believers are regularly trained to function as prayer ministers.

Bringing healing and wholeness to people's lives was central in the ministry of Jesus. Wholeness Ministries believes that His ministry of bringing healing and wholeness needs to be central to the ministry of the Church today. All believers are gifted by the Holy Spirit and called to use these gifts in ministry to others. Wholeness Ministries provides training and encouragement so that these God-given gifts come forth in people's lives.

The Style of Prayer Ministry

The Wholeness Ministries model is based on concepts that God has revealed to us over several years. This is one model for doing ministry. As with all "models for ministry," we urge that you seek God and ask Him to reveal how He would have you use this model or incorporate parts of it into your prayer style.

Our style of prayer ministry is based on the following concepts.

- We know and acknowledge that God is the Healer; He chooses to use us as we yield to Him in obedience.
- We pray in the name and authority of Jesus, with power from the Holy Spirit.
- We seek to see each person through God's eyes and heart and minister in the style of Jesus, with respect, gentleness, love and concern.
- We are sensitive to the need for privacy and confidentiality.
- We keep ministry sessions on track, but do not rush.

We have found that these concepts allow prayer teams to minister in many settings with diverse groups of people. Most prayer recipients are pleasantly surprised to find that the session is not frightening or mysterious, but rather under the control of the Holy Spirit.

Intercession

Wholeness Ministries was born as a result of the prayers of many people and continues because intercessors regularly seek God on behalf of this ministry. Intercession is crucial. It is in prayer that battles are won, it is in prayer that the soil of human hearts is prepared to receive the gospel and the healing touch of Jesus.

Any church or group that believes God is calling them to develop a prayer team ministry needs to gather a group of intercessors to wait on God's direction. As you pray, God will prepare and call those He wants to draw into prayer team ministry. He will also raise up additional intercessors and leadership as you continue to seek Him.

Starting a prayer team ministry with high hopes and detailed plans works only when the plans are God's specific plans for your body, not just copies of someone else's plan. God will tailor the ministry to meet the needs of the church and the community in which it is located, if leaders are faithful to seek His plans. Intercession is the key to knowing the heart of God for your body.

> *In the same way, the Spirit helps us in our weakness. We do not know what we ought to pray for, but the Spirit himself intercedes for us with groans that words cannot express. And he who searches our hearts knows the mind of the Spirit, because the Spirit intercedes for the saints in accordance with God's will. Romans 8:26-27*

> *Do not be anxious about anything, but in everything, by prayer and petition, with thanksgiving, present your requests to God. Philippians 4:6*

> *Again, I tell you that if two of you on earth agree about anything you ask for, it will be done for you by my Father in heaven. For where two or three come together in my name, there am I with them.   Matthew 18:19-20*

The Task Force

Within the church setting a Task Force needs to be established that meets weekly to pray for God's vision and direction in conducting the day-to-day business of the ministry.

Task force members also determine the training to be offered to prayer teams, interview new prayer team members, provide guidance and correction for prayer teams, pray with team members that need personal ministry, and match people requesting prayer with a prayer team. The selection of task force members must be done prayerfully to ensure mature leadership for these important functions and any others that are appropriate for your group.

Within the church setting, a task force is generally established under the leadership of the Senior Pastor or the Associate Pastor assigned the responsibility for prayer ministry. It is crucial that all prayer ministry leaders and prayer ministers be submitted to the local church and its leadership.

Settings for Prayer Ministry

Prayer teams can function in a variety of settings within the local church. We offer these possibilities, which can be tailored to your church body.

1. *Sunday morning at the close of each service*, either someplace in the regular gathering place, or in a room that is set aside for prayer ministry.

2. *Sunday evening in a service or in home groups*, depending upon the format for your body.

3. *Midweek service or midweek home groups*, depending upon the format for your body.

4. *Midweek ministry time*, where prayer teams are available to individuals on a first come, first served basis at a designated time and location for 20 to 30 minute prayer times.

5. *Special events*, such as training seminars or conferences as the schedule permits.

6. *By appointment* for extended prayer times over several weeks with mature, trained people in a private setting.

Section 9: Recruiting and Training Prayer Teams

Introduction to Becoming a Prayer Team Member

While we believe that anyone can pray for another person, we have a responsibility to those who are coming to receive prayer from this ministry to assure them that the people praying for them have been trained and equipped and can be trusted. We do not want to wound the wounded out of our ignorance.

We are not seeking to build an "elite" group of prayers. We are, however, building and training prayer warriors who are willing to go to the front lines, wherever the lines may be: work, school, neighborhoods, hospitals, homes, youth groups, home groups, Sunday Schools, and at church in any gathering.

We want to build special teams for special needs. We want to train and build groups of prayer warriors to work within the church framework to minister whenever and wherever needed.

This is a ministry we take seriously, and we must also take our responsibility seriously when it comes to a decision as to who can be placed on the prayer ministry teams. In order to provide some protection to those who come for prayer, we must use wisdom and good discernment when placing people on teams.

Why We Pray In Teams

This ministry teaches and strongly urges you to pray and minister with people as teams. Most of the time our teams are made up of two individuals, but occasionally there will be three members. If it is okay with the prayer recipient we may have someone who is new to this style of ministry sitting in on the session to observe and intercede.

While it is true that as Christians we can pray anytime, anywhere and for anyone we feel led, and while it is true that there are Biblical examples of individuals who apparently travelled and ministered alone (Philip in Acts 8), there is a strong Biblical case for ministering in teams.

- Mark 6:7 "Calling the Twelve to him, he sent them out two by two and gave them authority over evil spirits."

- Mark 11:1 ". . . Jesus sent two of his disciples . . ."

- Mark 14:13 "So he sent two of his disciples . . ."

- Luke 10:1 "After this the Lord appointed seventy-two others and sent them two by two ahead of him to every town and place where he was about to go."

- Acts 3Peter and John minister to the crippled beggar

- Acts 8:14The church in Jerusalem sent Peter and John to Samaria

- Acts 13:2 "While they were worshiping the Lord and fasting, the Holy Spirit said, 'Set apart for me Barnabas and Saul for the work to which I have called them.'

- Acts 15:40 "but Paul chose Silas and left, commended by the brothers to the grace of God."

   Again, I tell you that if two of you on earth agree about anything you ask for, it will be done for you by my Father in heaven. For where two or three come together in my name, there am I with them Matthew 18:19-20

There are many advantages to praying in teams.

- **Intercession:** As one member of the team interviews or prays for the prayer recipient the other member can be interceding on behalf of both of them.

- **Discernment:** The team member who is being quiet is often the one to hear specific direction from the Lord. They can also learn a lot by observing what is happening while ministry is taking place.

- **Confirmation:** Often when we pray one person will express what they think the Lord is saying and the prayer recipient or other team member will confirm it.

- **Accountability:** Praying as teams has a built in accountability to it. There are at least two witnesses to every thing that is said and done. If someone does something questionable or prays in a way that is not Biblical or beneficial, it can be checked by the other team member immediately.

- **Learning:** Each of us has had a unique journey with the Lord and we bring to the ministry session all that God has taught us along the way. We often learn by listening to each other in sessions and sharing with one another afterwards.

- **Blend of Gifts:** God has also equipped each of us with the gifts and talents He desires us to have. We are not alike. Paul says we are like different parts of the body (1 Corinthians 12:12-30). Each is necessary and each has a specific function in the body. Often it is the unique blend of gifts among team members that brings effective ministry.

- **Debriefing:** A team member gives you someone to debrief and pray with in regards to ministry sessions without violating the confidentiality necessary for this ministry.

- **Friendship:** It is a wonderful bonus of prayer ministry that strong friendships are formed as we minister side by side in Jesus name.

Ministry Requirements

Criteria for Prayer Ministers

1. To serve on a Prayer Ministry Team it is necessary to satisfy the following criteria:

    *   The individual must be a born-again, Spirit-filled Christian

    *   They have been baptized.

    *   They attend worship service regularly.

    *   They demonstrate spiritual growth.

    *   Their lifestyle demonstrates Christian witness.

    *   They have a teachable spirit.

    *   They believe God is calling them to this ministry.

    *   They are active within their local church.

2. The individual must attend training workshops as offered on the:

    *   Basic Entry Level-(Prayer Ministry Training Manual)

    *   Intermediate & Advanced Level (Supplementary material on specific topics)

3. The individual must be willing to make a commitment to serve on a prayer team at specific times and settings.

4. The candidate must be willing to complete a Prayer Ministry Questionnaire (See page G1 for a sample.) and an interview session with the Task Force. Refer to page C1 for the interview questions and to page B1 for more about the actual interview process.

When an individual requests to be placed on a prayer team one of the first things to do is ask them to observe a team ministering to an individual. Ask them not to participate but merely to observe and later give their reactions. This is important because it can tell much about their willingness to place themselves under authority and follow the directions they are given. This also gives them an opportunity to determine if they wish to become involved in prayer ministry using the style and method God is developing in your local congregation.

Occasionally, you may have an individual on one of your teams who ministers in a style that is offensive or inconsistent with what God is doing in your particular setting. This most likely is a result of models they have been exposed to in their past or experiences they have had while receiving ministry. It is the responsibility of leadership to lovingly confront and talk through what has been observed and bring correction where needed. If the method or style is sufficiently offensive and they will not change or modify their behavior then they should not be allowed to be on an officially recognized prayer team. This may sound harsh but we have a tremendous responsibility not to further "wound the wounded," but to do all we can to foster healing and wholeness.

Basic Preparation for the Prayer Ministry Teams

There are basic steps that need to become a part of the life of a prayer ministry team member. This doesn't happen overnight but is a process that takes place over time.

Priority

Prayer must be like breathing. We don't think about it—-we just do it! Commitment to praying for others needs to be high on the priority list of what we do. Examples are:

- Have your schedule open to allow for time to pray for others.

- Arrange for child-care if necessary so the time can be uninterrupted.

Preparation

If you are going to be effective in ministry there must be time spent in preparation, which is essential. You must set aside time to:

Prepare your heart

- Spend necessary time in confession and repentance.

- Spend time in the study of God's Word.

- Spend time in prayer.

Prepare your spirit

- Put on the Armor of God.

- Spend time daily in praise and worship.

Prepare for warfare

- Call upon God.

- Claim the authority and power given by God.

- Take up the weapons of the warfare.

- Set out to establish victory and peace.

Practice

Look to see what the Father is doing. Practice increases your faith as you see God at work and it also strengthens you and helps you to grow.

- Go in obedience.

- Go in faith.

- Do the stuff!

Perseverance

Don't give in or give up! Keep going personally in your own prayer life and in your prayer ministry. Even if the waters get deep and it would be easier to give up, remember that when you persevere you will receive a great benefit, not to mention the incredible damage you do to push back the kingdom of darkness.

How Ministry Teams Function

The following is a model of how the prayer teams can function in a church setting. With some modification this model can be easily adapted to your particular church setting. Based on time available you may need to eliminate some of these steps.

Prayer Ministry Procedures

1. Ideally meet for prayer 15 minutes prior to beginning of service.

2. Check in with the prayer ministry team coordinator.

3. Pick up an ID badge.

4. At the close of each service, teams come to a designated location when called to pray with people.

5. The Pastors or prayer team coordinator will direct prayer recipient to teams.

6. Proceed to designated prayer areas: These could be:

   - Prayer Room

   - Back of Sanctuary or side aisles

   - Designated area of adjoining building

   - Front of Sanctuary

Midweek Evening Prayer Ministry Procedures

In this model we utilize a room which is set up with 5-7 groups of chairs, with 3-4 chairs per group. Each team, which consists of two or three people, is assigned one of these groups. A building entry is used as a reception area where those coming for prayer are greeted by the Prayer Coordinator and given prayer request slips to complete. See page A1 for a sample prayer slip. The slips are returned to the coordinator who then brings each individual into the prayer room and introduces them to an available prayer team. In addition to a large prayer room, private offices are available for sensitive cases.

Note:

All that is spoken by the prayer recipient is confidential and must not be told to others. This is a safe place for people who are coming and trusting, so let's keep it safe.

Guidelines for Prayer Team Members

1. Depend on the leading of the Holy Spirit and the Scriptures to give you the wisdom you need in praying with people. Don't rush in and start praying!

2. Expect any of the gifts of the Holy Spirit to be manifested as needed.

3. Take control from the start. Begin by saying, "Hello, my name is... What's yours?" Make them feel at ease and encourage them to talk. Keep the conversation to the point, however, and stop unnecessary digression. It may be helpful to say something like, "Let's stop and take a look at that."

4. Remain objective. As a prayer counselor, you must be able to control your emotions in order to help them receive ministry.

5. Listen attentively. You can learn a lot by "listening between the lines." Observe facial expressions, be sensitive to tone of voice and to what is left unsaid. For more on how to listen see page

6. Watch for common problem areas. Some familiar ones are feelings of fear, rejection, bitterness, and unforgiveness over past hurts.

7. Be straightforward with individuals receiving ministry. Don't try to skirt the issues, hoping they will get the point. Use simple language so they can clearly understand what you are saying.

8. Don't let them dwell on what another person may have done. They are the ones who have come for help, so direct the conversation back to them. This can be done by asking "And how did that make you feel?" or "What can I help you with?"

9. Concentrate on the immediate need because of the short time available. Do not attempt "in-depth" counseling.

10. Suggest professional counseling with a Christian counselor if they need more extensive counseling than you can offer. Have the names of some trusted Christian counselors and/or pastors available.

11. Show them love and acceptance. This is a basic need in everyone and many do not feel loved and accepted by God or by others.

12. Genuinely care about them. Do not treat them as a "case." Help them to see themselves as a worthwhile individual.

13. Offer mercy and compassion. Don't judge what they have done. Your goal is to help, not condemn.

14. Assure them of God's forgiveness. It is important that they learn to accept God's forgiveness and to forgive themselves.

15. Don't just tell them to pray. Lead them in prayer and ask the Lord for answers to all their needs.

16. Keep all information shared with you strictly confidential. Sometimes Christians are misled into spreading gossip under the guise of sharing a prayer concern with others.

17. Recognize and acknowledge their free will. Not everyone who needs help wants help. Many people do not want to change, even when they are miserable and hurting.

18. Do not assume responsibility for their life. A momentary plea for help is not an invitation to manage their life permanently.

19. Realize that you will make some mistakes. Be conscientious before God in fulfilling the responsibility of a prayer minister to the best of your ability. If a mistake is made, ask God's forgiveness, rectify the mistake, if possible, and release it to the Lord.

For further information on building and training teams see page M-1.

Section 10: Generational Healing

Introduction to Generational Healing

This section deals with being under the influence of past generations and how that influence could hurt us today. Most of us are aware of passages like this one in Exodus 34:6-7 which says:

> *"Yahweh, God of tenderness and compassion, slow to anger, rich in faithful love and constancy, maintaining His faithful love to thousands, forgiving fault, crime, and sin, yet letting nothing go unchecked, and punishing the parents' fault in the children and in the grandchildren, to the third and fourth generation."*

There has always been this awareness that what has gone wrong in past generations can influence us. We seem to know by experience that something is wrong. There is evil in the world. There is some kind of evil, or sin, or weakness in us that is more than us, and we need a Savior to release us and to free us from the effects of that sin.

The sins of the past generations and their weaknesses affect all of us in some way. Some of it is very understandable, like the way we learn in our homes how to relate to one another. For instance, if there is violence in the home, it tends to go on, generation-to-generation. To stop or change this we need to be set free from those destructive patterns that we learn in the home.

What we are talking about is something more than that in us. The wonderful thing is that if we touch on something that is really deep and profound, and we pray about that, often people will say, with just one prayer, "I felt something lift off. I don't know what it was, but there was a kind of heaviness that lifted off, and now I feel light and happy. I have never felt that way before. There was something there, but whatever it was, it is gone."

There is a great deal of mystery in all of this. People have been trying to figure it out for centuries. Remember the man born blind? The people around were saying, *"Now, who sinned? He sinned, or did his parents sin, that he should be born blind?"* There is always this effort to say, "Why is this happening now? What went wrong, and who do we blame?" We're always looking for somebody to blame. Jesus answer was, "This happened that the glory of God might be made manifest," because Jesus already knew that he was going to heal him.

Sometimes in ministry we have exhausted every track of personal sin only to find trouble still besetting the person's life. In time we began to understand that some of the causes came from outside the person's own guilt or sin nature. We discover that sin and its effects were passed down through family lines.

In part we see at work the law of sowing and reaping. Reaping for sin is seldom immediate. It is also never without increase, since all seeds of sin ripen to produce thirty, sixty or a hundredfold. The principle in Matthew 13:8 of the seed and what it produces applies here also. Time, though not the only factor, remains a major reason why children reap what fathers and grandparents and great-grandparents have sown.

It may seem unfair that unborn children, years later, are required to suffer the effects of the law for sins committed by ancestors who may even be unknown to them. Of course, it is not fair. God is fair, but since sin entered God's world, life is not fair. God has worked from the beginning to re-establish His justice through the cross of Christ. Whenever men will not repent, and by that fail to give God access, men must reap generation-to-generation whatever is sown, however unfair that may be to the unborn.

What we have discovered is that destruction often rains upon people when nothing inside them any longer attracts it. Then we begin to see that generational sin may be the cause.

Sometimes when you begin to look at the family history you see patterns. Sometimes divorce runs rampant. Addictions like alcohol, drugs, sex may go back generations.

So what is this evil that we experience as the result of past generations? There are several levels of this evil and four of these levels are covered in this study.

Genetic Predispositions

The first is that there are just purely human, natural, genetic predispositions toward various kinds of sickness. We recognize this when we go to the doctor's office and they ask us to fill out a chart: "Did your parents have cancer, did they have arthritis…?" We recognize that these things do go through the generations and that some people have a predisposition to types of sickness. Some have a predisposition to breast cancer, some to sickle cell anemia. So it is not a spiritual thing at all but it is something that apparently goes down through the genes. Medical researchers are also finding that there are dispositions to various temperamental aspects of our lives. Not only do physical conditions descend; personality and behavioral tendencies do so as well.

Which of your kids can you look at and say he/she is just like his father/mother? On my father's side of the family there is a predisposition to be adventurous. We are risk-takers, we like challenges, we become bored quickly if there is not some new challenge waiting for us. There is a good and bad side to this. We have mannerisms and habits that could have come from no other source than our family line. I am very much like my father and I see traits in my daughter that I see in myself and saw in my father and grandfather. Of my three children she is definitely the entrepreneur, risk-taker, adventurous one. Once a challenge has been conquered, maintenance becomes boring; we are constantly looking for the next challenge or adventure.

The good news is that we can pray that God break all these genetic predispositions to sickness and to traits that are harmful or destructive. It's just like praying for healing: we can ask God through the power of the Holy Spirit to break that and to break us free-not only us, but our children, and their children. Break it right now and stop it!

So it is like physical healing going on in the very genes of our bodies, in the chromosomes and all those amazing things that the scientists are now discovering are in our bodies that predispose us to various things.

Some of these are gifts. For example, to be creative, artistic or intellectual is a good thing. That part is there in the genes, so we are not just looking at bad things. We are looking at things for which we also praise God. It's like most things in life. There is light and there is dark and the very gifts that I have I also usually have a corresponding weakness. People who are creative tend to live in the imaginations. They are often not practical.

Spiritual Weaknesses

Now we have discussed the weakness that comes down to us on the physical plane and what we can do about that, asking God to break it. There is also weakness that comes down through the spiritual plane. This issue is not addressed in most churches. There is much talk about praying for forgiveness for particular sins committed by an individual, but very little discussion about the generational or the group experience of sin and what to do about the sins and weaknesses that come down through family patterns.

Francis MacNutt tells the story of a family that he knows who discovered their eight year old son beating his head against a wall and talking about ending his life. The family had no idea where this originated and did not see any similar behavior in the boy's sibling. Over time Francis discovered that the boy's grandfather and two other relatives from his parents' generation had committed suicide-three suicides in his parents' immediate families.

Now you cannot prove that the behavior of this boy is definitely linked to the suicides of a past generation, but when you see a destructive pattern over a period of time it is worthwhile to seek the Lord over the need for the healing of the generations.

We are also aware that there is a predisposition to alcoholism. This is a major issue in our society. Within my own family line as I reflect back over what I have observed I recognize this weakness.

Demonic Influences

From our experience it would appear that there is something in the genes that influences us spiritually. There are several very obvious things that do influence us. One is the demonic. And again most churches don't deal with the demonic so they will not be regarded as superstitious. Our experience is that demonic infestation can be carried on through the generations. What happens to one person, if the child is not protected, can pass on to the next generation mysteriously. It is almost like a disease passed from generation to generation.

It is fascinating that the traditional Catholic baptismal rite has an exorcism in it. That seems pretty primitive-you have a six-week old baby, and you are praying an exorcism. This baby has never done anything, but it was recognition in the early church that these things could be passed on in a pagan atmosphere, if the child is not protected. It is not something recent that we have made up, it goes back generations.

Francis MacNutt tells the story of praying with a committed Christian woman and discovering that one of the things that was wrong in her life was that she hated men. They discovered that she was the daughter of a prostitute. As they actually started praying, there was a demonic manifestation, and the demon identified itself as "hatred of men." Apparently it came from the mother who hated men. This demonic interference was passed on to the daughter very early on, probably in the womb, so they prayed that she be cut free from this hatred of men.

Obviously we want to be set free from anything that might be present in our lives. Things can just come down, almost like a disease, from generation to generation. When we pray for that it is very simple. We pray almost like deliverance that this person be set free from any demonic interference that has come down through the generations.

> *"By the Sword of the Spirit, and in the Name of Jesus Christ, we set you free from anything that has come down from past generations upon you now. In the Name of Jesus Christ, be set free from all that. And not only you, but also all your family, and all your children, and grandchildren that you will be set free. We command any satanic interference, now, to leave and to go to Jesus Christ."*

Curses

Idolatry Deut 5:9-10 *"You shall not bow down to them or worship them; for I, the Lord your God, am a jealous God, punishing the children for the sin of the fathers to the third and fourth generation of those who hate me, but showing love to a thousand generations, of those who love me and keep my commandments."*

Sexual Immorality Acts 15:19-20 *"It is my judgment, therefore, that we should not make it difficult for the Gentiles who are turning to God. Instead we should write to them, telling them to abstain from food polluted by idols, from sexual immorality, from the meat of strangled animals and from blood."*

Three main causes of generational curses are:
1. If the family has been involved in the occult, especially if there have been witches or warlocks in the family.
2. If the family itself has been cursed by someone else.
3. If the family has been deeply involved in some kind of habitual sinful activity.

These generational curses can have two effects. **One**, great blessings may simply be blocked. The curse forms a barrier that needs to be broken so that God's blessing can flow upon our family. **Second**, multiple disasters sometimes seem to target a family. What prominent family in the United States comes immediately to your mind when you think of tragedy afflicting several generations? Certainly in our society there is a possibility that the Kennedy's are cursed. It seems more than just coincidence that there appears to be a pattern of evil that affects that family. It looks like with all the people who are killed violently in that family and the tragedy in that family that there is something beyond coincidence. You cannot prove this, but if there is a pattern of evil, that affects a family, all kinds of evil-anywhere from violent deaths to more financial disaster than you would expect-then perhaps there is a curse there.

The ancient Greeks even named a goddess, Nemesis, to represent the personal force that harasses and pursues a family to destroy it. When we use words to describe this phenomenon, like uncanny, or when members of a family suffer from some foreboding or a fear of death, they are recognizing intuitively that a power beyond the normal seems to govern their family's "fate."

When someone in the family has been involved in the occult it has effects for many generations. If someone in our ancestry did something such as consecrate the family to Satan, the disastrous results continue until the curse is broken. Dr. Charles Kraft tells the story of a woman who came to him for prayer. In the course of ministering to her she confessed that she had made a covenant with Satan. If Satan would give her wealth, she would give him her firstborn. She became very wealthy but her firstborn son was a mess.

Whatever shape it takes, whether deaths, divorces, financial losses, illnesses or accidents, such coincidences happen so often that one can hardly miss seeing a design behind it all.

There is not a lot taught about this in our seminaries or in our Western churches. It is generally regarded as superstition. In our experience it is not superstition at all. There are curses that are pronounced upon a family that can affect people in the family, and they don't even know it. I found in going to Romania that the gypsies were very aware of these things. They are much more aware of these things than we are. They are very aware that witches can put curses on a family and they may not even know it. Even at a great distance you can be affected. It was not unusual for them to ask for prayer specifically for curses to be broken that were in their family line.

> A number of years ago I was at a Christian camp and a family asked me to come pray for their young son who was about 8 years old. He was totally out of control and they were at there wits end. Nothing that they tried to help bring some discipline or order in his life was working. They told me he would not sit still to be prayed for so I went over to their cabin late one evening when he was asleep. The mother and father stood in the doorway and I went into the bedroom, knelt down by the bed, placed my hand on him and began to pray. For awhile nothing happened. I felt prompted to ask the parents if there was any American Indian in their ancestry and the mother said that her parents were Native Americans. I laid my hand back on the boy and prayed that if anything had been passed down from previous generations that it would be cut off and leave.

> Suddenly he began to violently thrash around in the bed; this lasted for about 4-5 seconds and then he became completely still. During this time he never woke up so I prayed a little bit more and then left. The next morning the mother and father came over to me and they were both radiant and excited about the change in their son. He was a completely different child. They could not believe the change in him.

I have returned to this camp over the years and watched this boy grow into a fine young man, doing well in school. He has even taken some mission trips overseas and seems very interested in pursuing work in some form of ministry.

Let me encourage you that there are ways to pray that are fairly simple.

> *"If there is a curse, in the Name of Jesus Christ, in the power of the Spirit, I set you free! And whatever curse is upon this family, I break it, and I declare it null and void now in the Name of Jesus Christ who sets you free. I command any satanic influence, any effects, I command them all to depart in the Name of Jesus Christ, and for you to be set free."*

Sometimes when you pray this prayer the person feels an immediate release. They didn't even know it was there but they have always felt oppressed or depressed and it just lifts off. Sometimes when we pray for a group different individuals in the group feel these things just lift off.

We can discover and stop generational patterns of sin by direct action in prayer. I have seen long-time Christians suffer from generational patterns until someone by God's grace prayed effectively to stop that destruction.

Prayers for generational sin, like prayers for conversion, are normally one-time prayers. Whoever voices this prayer must know his authority in Christ as a child of the King. Powers of darkness do not yield territory to halfhearted prayers. This prayer to stop generational sin is not merely for healing. Nor is it only defensive, as though stopping the encroachments of darkness were enough. It is aggressive warfare on the march to recover lost souls from the grip of darkness.

A prayer we often use to pray over a group is The Deliverance Prayer in Appendix I-1 of this book, "Learning To Do What Jesus Did." We have found this to be very effective in freeing people from generational curses.

How Do We Pray?

1. In prayer we call for the healing of Jesus to flow back through family bloodlines throughout their history, by forgiveness washing away the ground of Satan's attack.
2. Whatever patterns we have seen, we specifically ask for our Lord to destroy it. In some cases we are led to rebuke the powers of darkness and to command them to leave.
3. We ask God to send His angels about every member of the family to protect each one and to bring each one out of darkness into light.

Appendix A: Prayer Request Slip

PRAYER MINISTRY INFORMATION

DATE _____

NAME _____

ADDRESS _____

CITY _____ STATE _____ ZIP _____

PHONE _____

PRAYER REQUEST _____

_____

_____

FOLLOW UP _____

_____

_____

CONTACT PERSON _____

Learning to Do What Jesus Did

Appendix B:How to Use the Interview Sheet

Purpose

The Wholeness Ministries Interview Sheet has been developed as a tool to help us get to know people who come to us and express the desire to be a part of our prayer team ministry. In most cases the indi-viduals who express a desire to be a part of this ministry are indeed being led by the Holy Spirit, but once in a while that is not the case. We also find that those who come to us are not equally equipped.

Some already have years of experience, while for others prayer ministry is brand new. It is an awe-some privilege to pray for someone and have the joy of watching the Holy Spirit move compassion-ately and powerfully in a person's life. Prayer team members need to have compassion and sensitivity for the person for whom they are praying and a desire to discern what the Father is doing and what He wants them to do in any given situation.

Team members must be willing to seek to keep a clean heart before the Lord, be able to function as a part of a team, have a solid understanding of Biblical truth, be able to keep things they learn during ministry sessions confidential and truly believe that God is calling them into this type of ministry.

Procedure

At least two members of our leadership team conduct an interview. Usually one person will ask the questions while the other person records the answers. Our policy is to have the person being inter-viewed complete one of our Prayer Ministry Questionnaires (see page G-1) and return it to us before the oral interview takes place. We always begin the time together with prayer. The interview itself simply consists of asking the questions on the Interview Sheet and listening to and writing down the responses. It is very informal and every member of the leadership team who is present is free to ask additional questions in response to what the individual says.

After the Interview Sheet is completed we go over the recommended reading list (see page D-1) and check off those specific books on the list that the person has read. We also ask them to tell us of any seminars, classes, conferences etc. that they have attended which have helped prepare them for prayer ministry. We keep the copy that we have checked, and then give them a copy for their own reference. We strongly encourage our team members to keep reading and keep learning.

The Prayer Ministry Questionnaire will have been read by the members of the leadership team be-fore the interview. If it brought up any concerns or questions, they are discussed at this time. If the leader-ship team feels that the person needs to have prayer ministry or deal with some issues in their own life, we offer them the opportunity to meet with a team in the near future. Each individual is different and discernment is needed. Just because they have issues to deal with does not necessarily mean that they can not be on a team. We are all in the process of being transformed and need to ex-tend grace to one another. However if you feel a caution or a check in your spirit, then do indeed be cautious.

Next we go over our release agreement (see page E-1) and have the person being interviewed and two members of our leadership team sign it. The person being interviewed is given a copy of this agreement. The Interview Sheet, the Prayer Ministry Questionnaire, the book list, and the release agreement all go in a file which we keep in the Wholeness Ministries office.

When the interview is completed the person is simply told that the leadership team will discuss their becoming a prayer team member at their next meeting and then be in contact with them. No matter what, we always try to be encouraging to people.

If for any reason we determine that we are not yet ready to put the individual on our teams, we encourage them towards growth in their Christian walk by making very specific recommendations. Maybe they need to establish a daily time with the Lord or find a place to fellowship and be nurtured in the faith. Maybe there are issues or attitudes in their life that they need to pray over and work through. The possibility of future involvement in the ministry is left open.

Most people will however be brought onto the teams. We make three designations as to their involvement. If we feel that they have the heart for this ministry and God is calling them into it, but they do not have much experience or training, we bring them on as beginners. They are assigned to be the third member of a prayer team. They are quiet during the ministry sessions and are there to observe and intercede. When we know the person fairly well, when trust has been built, when we have established that they have a considerable amount of training and experience and when we feel that they can take the leadership role in prayer sessions, they are then designated as a leader. Everyone else in between, who are not truly beginners or yet ready to be leaders, are designated as intermediates.

Reasons for the Questions

The questions on the interview sheet are designed:

- To tell about the person's testimony and background as a believer

- To determine what their current walk with the Lord is like

- To determine what teaching and experience they have had

- To determine what teaching and experience they have not had

- To see if they are comfortable with the style of ministry we use

- To help us match them with people who need prayer

- To determine some of their basic Christian doctrine to be sure there are no major misconceptions or conflicts

- To reveal their heart

The Unexpected Reward

When we started using this interview sheet we made a wonderful discovery. Each of the interviews we did proved to be a very special time. Everybody was blessed. It is always uplifting to hear a person's story and learn how the Lord has and is moving in their life. We learned interesting things even about those people we had known for many years. It provides the opportunity to focus in on one individual and really listen to them. We have also learned that it provides that individual with our undivided attention and they often take advantage of the chance to ask us questions. Normally by the end of these sessions everyone is feeling richly blessed and grateful for the time together.

Appendix C: Prayer Team Interview Sheet

Date of Interview_____

Name_____ Birth Date_____

Home Address_____

Home Phone_____

Employer_____

Work Address_____

Work Phone_____

Any comments about work_____

_____

_____

Marital Status_____ Spouse's Name_____

      Children's Name(s)   Age(s)

      _____   _____

      _____   _____

      _____   _____

      _____   _____

      _____   _____

Are you a mother/father in-law?_____

Are you a grandparent?_____

Age you received Christ_____   Baptized_____

Church Background_____

_____

Current Church Membership_____

_____

Share your testimony with us about how you came to know the Lord Jesus Christ.

How did you come to experience the presence and the power of the Holy Spirit?

Tell us about your current walk with the Lord.

Are prayer and Bible reading a part of your daily life?

In your opinion, how does a person discern God's will in their life?

Have you personally experienced:
Physical healing?_____
Inner healing?_____
Deliverance?_____

What experience have you had with the gifts of the Holy Spirit?

What other types of ministry have you been involved in?

Share with us why you feel God is calling you into this ministry.

Tell us about your prayer team experience so far.

What areas of ministry do you feel you understand best?

What areas of ministry do you feel you most need more training in?

Have you or someone close to you had to deal with:(circle)

Alcoholism	Drugs
Rebellious children	Terminally ill
Chronically ill	Disabilities
Marriage problems	Sexual struggles
Depression	Fear
Rejection	Mental illness
Abuse	Cult background
Un-saved mates	Bitterness
Raising grandchildren	Family member in prison
Elderly parents	Demonic
Low self esteem	

Share with us any area of struggle, crisis, or victory in your life that might be used of the Lord to help minister to others.

What must a person do to be saved?

How does one receive the Holy Spirit?

What is your experience when praying for those in need of physical healing?

What is your understanding of inner healing?

What is your experience with deliverance?

What is the role of praise in a Christian's life?

What does it mean to intercede in prayer?

How do you think Jesus views our culture?

What is Jesus' heart for the lost?

What is Jesus' heart for the hurting Christian?

What is Jesus specifically asking you to do with your life?

Appendix D: Recommended Reading

Disclaimer

Each person who is accepted as a prayer minister in Wholeness Ministries is provided with a recommended reading list that includes the following disclaimer.

Read all material seeking the Holy Spirit's discernment. The opinions and conclusions expressed in these books are those of the authors and do not necessarily reflect in every case the positions of Wholeness Ministries.

Basic Reading List

Physical Healing

- Francis MacNutt; Healing

- Francis MacNutt; The Power to Heal

- Norma Dearing; The Healing Touch

Inner Healing

- David Seamands; Healing for Damaged Emotions

- Charles Kraft; Deep Wounds, Deep Healing

- John & Paula Sandford; The Transformation of the Inner Man

- John & Paula Sandford; Healing the Wounded Spirit

Spiritual Warfare

- Dean Sherman; Spiritual Warfare

- Francis Frangipane; The Three Battlegrounds

Deliverance

- Charles Kraft; Defeating Dark Angels

- Francis MacNutt; Deliverance From Evil Spirits

Intercession

- Cindy Jacobs; <u>Possessing the Gates of the Enemy</u>

- Dutch Sheets; <u>Intercessory Prayer</u>

<u>Further Recommended Reading</u>

World View

- Charles Kraft; <u>Christianity With Power</u>

- Don Williams; <u>Signs, Wonders, and the Kingdom of God</u>

- Bill Johnson; <u>When Heaven Invades Earth</u>

Prayer

- Richard Foster; <u>Prayer</u>

- Jack W. Hayford; <u>Prayer Is Invading the Impossible</u>

Resting in the Spirit

- Francis MacNutt; <u>Overcome by the Spirit</u>

The Gift of Tongues

- Jack W. Hayford; <u>The Beauty of Spiritual Language</u>

Listening to the Father

- Cindy Jacobs; <u>The Voice of God</u>

- Henri Nouwen; <u>The Life of the Beloved</u>

- Michael Evans; <u>Why Not Waste Time With God?</u>

- Jack Frost; <u>Experiencing the Father's Embrace</u>

Freedom from Bondage

- Neil Anderson; <u>A Way of Escape</u>

- Don Williams; <u>Jesus and Addiction</u>

Self Image (Our Identity in Christ)

- Neil Anderson; <u>Victory Over The Darkness</u>

- Neil Anderson; <u>The Bondage Breaker</u>

- Brother Lawrence; <u>The Practice of the Presence of God</u>

- Brennan Manning; <u>The Ragamuffin Gospel</u>

- Brennan Manning; <u>Abba's Child</u>

Personal Growth and Enrichment

- Francis Frangipane; <u>Holiness, Truth and the Presence of God</u>

- Brennan Manning; <u>Ruthless Trust: The Ragamuffin's Path to God</u>

- Brennan Manning; <u>The Relentless Tenderness of Jesus</u>

- Thomas Kelley; <u>A Testament of Devotion</u>

Appendix E: Release Agreement for Team Members

This ministry is called PRAYER MINISTRY. It is not professional counseling. We are not professional counselors and are not licensed or insured as such. We work with people only as they choose to work with us. We do not charge for our services.

God has seen fit to work with and through us in moving people toward wholeness. It is, therefore, our expectation that He will use us to help them, but we cannot promise results. We can only promise that we will do our best to work with God for their good and God's glory.

What usually happens in this type of ministry is that God brings another degree of healing in each session. There is a move toward wholeness as we seek healing together. Seldom is this all that is necessary in order for a person to attain the complete freedom he/she and God desire. Sometimes it is advisable for the person to receive help from a professional counselor as well. It is also always advisable for the person to actively pursue spiritual disciplines such as church attendance, prayer, Bible study and worship along with the ministry.

It is imperative to keep confidential what ever is shared with us. Nothing will destroy this ministry faster than confidences which are shared with you and not kept sacred. We are required by law to report to appropriate persons two kinds of things:

- Any intent of a person to take harmful, dangerous, or criminal action against another person or against him/herself.

- Any act of child or elderly abuse or neglect.

If it appears that such notification needs to be given, that intention will be shared with the prayer recipient first.

In summary, we would like you to do the following:

1. Understand and agree to the above.

2. Be expectant, but not get upset or angry if all that you expect does not happen quickly.

3. Be patient with yourself and with God.

4. Be prayerful and open for growth and change under the guidance of the Holy Spirit.

5. Engage your will to work with the Holy Spirit and to move toward what God wants for the prayer recipient.

6. Forgive yourself if you make mistakes and release God if He doesn't do things the way you expect them to be done.

When you pray with someone you are praying under the covering of Wholeness Ministries. It is important to maintain the integrity of this ministry in all that we do. Should you find yourself in a situation that you are not comfortable in, please make this known to the leadership team. This could include things shared with you that by law require reporting to the appropriate authorities, a ministry situation where you do not feel comfortable being a part of that particular team, or if you feel like you are not experienced enough in the area being addressed and wish to withdraw yourself from the team.

I have read and understand the above information.

Signature:_____ Date: _____

Witness: _____ Date: _____

Witness: _____ Date: _____

Appendix F: How to Use the Prayer Ministry Questionnaire

As a Prayer Tool

The Prayer Ministry Questionnaire is a prayer tool for the prayer ministry team. It has been designed for "reading between the lines with the help of the Holy Spirit." God uses this tool to reveal things to the team and to bring focus to the ministry sessions.

Ideally you will have the completed Questionnaire prior to your first session. The prayer team members should spend time reading it prayerfully and carefully with a notebook and pen handy. Ask God to bring to your attention those questions that need to be asked and to help prioritize the questions. God can use very simple questions to reveal areas that need His touch.

An example of simple information that can be helpful occurred with a woman who had been ill for a long time and therefore appeared to be older than she was. When the prayer minister was drawn to the basic family information on the Questionnaire she realized that the woman had become a mother at a very young age. The question, "You were a very young mother, weren't you?" led to the revelation that she was pregnant at the time of her marriage, which occurred while she was still in high school. This had led to lots of resentment as her friends went away to college and returned with stories of fun and success. God brought significant healing as she forgave her husband, her friends and herself and she was not further wounded by lots of painful questions.

We do not have to pry and probe into very sensitive areas or go for all the gory details. Nor do we need to pursue every question on the form with the same vigilance. The Holy Spirit is faithful to reveal the starting place for each ministry session as we seek Him and then to lead us through the ministry time.

God may also call you to use the Questionnaire as a prayer guide between ministry sessions. He doesn't call us to wrestle with their problems or to get under them, but rather to lift them in prayer. This time spent in intercession can be one of the "costs" of prayer ministry. It can also be a rewarding time of blessing when God gives real insight into the person and their needs and into His plan for bringing healing to the person. He can also reveal areas in our life that need healing as we intercede on behalf of the other person. Praying over the Questionnaire can be a "win-win" situation.

To Identify Broken Relationships

With Other People

God's plan for man was to have relationship with him in the Garden of Eden and for Adam and Eve to have a relationship with each other. The accumulation of centuries of willful choices and sin has resulted in breaks in man's relationship with God and in people's relationships with one another. Much of the Prayer Ministry Questionnaire is designed to reveal broken relationships and the need for forgiveness to be extended and/or received. As Jack Hayford says in his book The Power and Blessing, "The spirit of unforgiveness takes a sure and tortuous toll on our bodies and souls." Jack W. Hayford, The

Power and Blessing, (Wheaton, IL., Victor Books, 1994) pp. 75-76. As prayer ministers, God frequently uses us to lead people from the tortures of unforgiveness.

The first pages of the Questionnaire ask for lots of personal history. As you talk through this section with the prayer recipient, you will often hear about broken family relationships. Some of these occurred early in life and have resulted in "yes" answers in the sections "What of the following applied to you during your childhood?" and "Which of the following have you struggled with in the past or are you struggling with presently?" The Holy Spirit can then guide you and the person through the process of identifying the root causes of pain and forgiving the person. All of the information in the chapter on Inner Healing and Forgiveness will be helpful in evaluating the Questionnaire (see page 5-1), but pay special attention to the section "What Are We Listening For?" (see page 5-20).

With God

The Questionnaire is also designed to reveal breaks in the relationship with God that come from reasons other than unforgiveness of other people or self. In particular the lengthy section on occult involvement identifies areas where the Word of God has been violated, since all occult activity is forbidden by scripture. (See page 6-8). It is idolatry—seeking after information and its associated power from a source or sources other than God. Occult involvement breaks the first commandment and invokes God's curse.

Those people who have been involved in occult practices have opened a door to oppressing spirits and broken fellowship with God. The person must close the door by a positive act of faith and then deal with the symptoms as is necessary. (See page 6-15) for details on how to close the door.)

The section on Moral Climate in the first 18 years of life can also identify possible breaks with God that come from extreme legalistic or permissive backgrounds. When the parent's style was not balanced, the child can get the idea that God is not balanced. In particular, if the person's relationship with their father was poor or indifferent, they may assume that God is indifferent to their needs or that He wants them to suffer. God may need to bring healing to their understanding of His nature and character.

Other Uses

The Questionnaire may bring some generational issues to the surface. For example, if all of the women in the prayer recipient's family for the last three or four generations have been divorced or abused or mentally ill (or any other problem that has recurred) this may indicate some kind of curse or hex on the family that needs to be broken or the presence of familiar evil spirits that need to be sent to Jesus for Him to deal with them. The person may also be experiencing a great deal of fear about their own chances or those of their children or grandchildren for suffering in the way their mother and grandmother have suffered. Seek the guidance of the Holy Spirit in dealing with generational problems, as in all other areas of prayer ministry.

Self esteem issues may also come to the surface in discussing the Questionnaire. The section on renewing the mind (see page 6-16) can be very helpful for those who need to be fed truth about what God says about them, once inner healing issues have been covered in ministry sessions.

The Questionnaire can also be used to get ministry sessions back on track if the prayer recipient is wandering or having trouble staying focused on the purpose for gathering. Using information from their answers you can say something like, "I see that you are adopted. How do you feel about that?" or "I see that you have had several surgeries recently. Can you tell us a little about the reasons for this?" or other appropriate questions that get the person back to the reason for meeting to pray. Asking about questions that they did not answer can also be a method for getting the person back into the session.

If we place our faith and trust in God, rather than in the Questionnaire, it has unlimited potential for bringing issues to the surface that need healing.

WHOLENESS MINISTRIES

P.O. Box 80503
Bakersfield, Ca. 93380
PRAYER MINISTRY QUESTIONNAIRE

NAME_____ DATE_____

ADDRESS_____

CITY_____STATE_____ZIP_____TELEPHONE_____

AGE_____SEX____BIRTHPLACE_____

EDUCATION(highest grade completed)_____

ARE YOU CURRENTLY EMPLOYED AND/OR GOING TO SCHOOL?_____

IS THERE ANYTHING SIGNIFICANT ABOUT YOUR CURRENT OR PAST WORK OR
SCHOOL EXPERIENCE THAT WE SHOULD KNOW?_____
_____
_____

WERE YOU RAISED BY ANYONE OTHER THAN YOUR PARENTS?EXPLAIN?_____
_____
_____

ARE YOU ADOPTED?_____

HOW MANY CHILDREN IN YOUR CHILDHOOD FAMILY? _____

WHERE ARE YOU IN YOUR FAMILY LINE OF SIBLINGS? _____

RELATIONSHIP TO FATHER IN CHILDHOOD: GOOD____BAD____INDIFFERENT___

RELATIONSHIP TO MOTHER IN CHILDHOOD: GOOD____BAD___INDIFFERENT___

RELATIONSHIP TO SIBLINGS: GOOD___BAD____INDIFFERENT____

HAS THERE BEEN SIGNIFICANT CHANGE IN ANY OF THESE AT PRESENT?_____
_____
_____

WHAT OF THE FOLLOWING APPLIED TO YOU DURING YOUR CHILDHOOD? (Circle)

NIGHT TERRORS	BED WETTING	SLEEP WALKING
INCEST	NAIL BITING	UNHAPPY CHILDHOOD
STAMMERING	EXCESSIVE FEAR	FREQUENT ILLNESSES
LONELINESS	MOLESTATION	BROKEN HOME
REMOVED FROM HOME		PHYSICAL DISABILITIES
LEARNING DISABILITIES		SERIOUS ILLNESSES
SEXUAL ENCOUNTERS		OTHER LEARNING PROBLEMS

STATUS OF PARENTS:

GOOD MARITAL RELATIONSHIP YES_____NO_____

ALCOHOLIC_____DRUGS_____DIVORCED_____SEPARATED_____DECEASED_____

PARENTS RELIGIOUS BACKGROUND_____

MARITAL STATUS:

MARRIED_____SEPARATED_____DIVORCED_____SINGLE_____WIDOWED_____

IF MARRIED, HOW MANY YEARS?_____

HOW MANY CHILDREN DO YOU HAVE?_____

WHAT IS YOUR CURRENT RELATIONSHIP WITH YOUR CHILDREN?_____

IF MARRIED BEFORE, HOW MANY TIMES?_____

WITH WHOM ARE YOU NOW LIVING?_____

PERSONAL HISTORY

CHURCH AFFILIATION PRESENT_____ PAST_____

BORN AGAIN_____DATE_____WATER BAPTISM_____DATE_____

INFANT BAPTISM YES____NO____

HOW OFTEN DO YOU CURRENTLY ATTEND CHURCH?_____

DO YOU HAVE REGULAR DEVOTIONS IN THE BIBLE?_____

DO YOU FIND PRAYER DIFFICULT?_____

DO YOU LISTEN TO MUSIC REGULARLY?_____

WHAT TYPE DO YOU ENJOY MOST?_____

HOW MANY HOURS OF TV DO YOU WATCH PER WEEK?_____

ARE YOU ADOPTED?_____

ARE YOU A VETERAN OF ANY FOREIGN WARS ? IF SO, WHICH_____

HAVE YOU DONE ANY FOREIGN TRAVEL?_____

DOES YOUR NAME HAVE ANY PARTICULAR SIGNIFICANCE AS TO FAMILY TRADITION OR CULTURAL/NATIONAL HERITAGE? _____

_____

DID YOUR PARENTS WISH YOU WERE OF THE OPPOSITE SEX?_____

IN YOUR OPINION, DID YOUR PARENTS WISH YOU HAD NEVER BEEN BORN?_____

HAVE THERE BEEN ANY MAJOR TRAUMAS IN YOUR LIFE?_____

IS THERE ANY PART OF YOUR LIFE (a large block of time) THAT YOU DON'T REMEMBER? _____

WHICH OF THE FOLLOWING HAVE YOU STRUGGLED WITH?

	PAST	NOW		PAST	NOW
Daydreaming	____	____	Lustful thoughts	____	____
Headaches	____	____	Thoughts of Inferiority	____	____
Worry	____	____	Thoughts of Inadequacy	____	____
Fantasy	____	____	Blasphemous thoughts	____	____
Insecurity	____	____	Obsessive thoughts	____	____
Doubts	____	____	Compulsive thoughts	____	____
Chronic pain	____	____	Dizzines	____	____
PMS	____	____			

WHICH OF THE FOLLOWING EMOTIONS HAVE YOU HAD DIFFICULTY CONTROLLING?

	PAST	NOW		PAST	NOW
Frustration	____	____	Fear of death	____	____
Anger	____	____	Fear of losing your mind	____	____
Loneliness	____	____	Fear of suicide	____	____
Anxiety	____	____	Fear of hurting loved ones	____	____
Bitterness	____	____	Depression	____	____
Hatred	____	____	Worthlessness	____	____

MORAL CLIMATE

DURING THE FIRST 18 YEARS OF YOUR LIFE, HOW WOULD YOU RATE THE MORAL ATMOSPHERE IN WHICH YOU WERE RAISED?_____

_____

	Overly Permissive	Permissive	Average	Strict	Overly Strict
Clothing	1	2	3	4	5
Sex	1	2	3	4	5
Dating	1	2	3	4	5
Movies	1	2	3	4	5
Music	1	2	3	4	5
Literature	1	2	3	4	5
Free Will	1	2	3	4	5
Drinking	1	2	3	4	5
Smoking	1	2	3	4	5
Church Attendance	1	2	3	4	5

DID YOU HAVE A KEEN INTEREST IN SEX BEFORE PUBERTY?_____

HAVE YOU VIEWED X-RATED MOVIES?_____

HAVE YOU LOOKED AT PORNOGRAPHY?_____

MEDICAL HISTORY

HAVE YOU EVER HAD OPERATIONS? IF SO, FOR WHAT REASON AND YOUR AGE AT THAT TIME?_____

_____

HAVE THERE BEEN MEDICAL TRAUMAS AND HOSPITALIZATION?_____

_____

HAVE YOU HAD AN ABORTION?_____

HAVE YOU HAD A MISCARRIAGE?_____

HOSPITALIZATION FOR EMOTIONAL ILLNESS? YES___NO___WHY?_____

_____

DIAGNOSIS, DATE, DISCHARGE STATUS_____

FORM OF TREATMENT_____

ARE YOU CURRENTLY UNDER THE CARE OF A DOCTOR, OR PSYCHIATRIST?_____

_____

ON DRUG THERAPY?_____DATE_____DISCHARGED_____

ARE YOU SUBJECT TO DEPRESSION?_____FREQUENCY_____

DURATION_____

DO YOU HAVE ANY ADDICTIONS OR CRAVINGS THAT YOU FIND DIFFICULT TO
CONTROL? (SWEETS,DRUGS,ALCOHOL,ETC.)_____

_____

ARE YOU AN ALCOHOLIC?_____HOW LONG?_____

HAVE YOU EVER USED STREET DRUGS?____HOW LONG?_____

ARE YOU STILL USING THEM?_____

HAVE YOU EVER MISUSED PRESCRIPTION DRUGS?_____HOW LONG?_____

OCCULT QUESTIONNAIRE

Have there been any occult contacts or involvement in your personal life or family history? Please check YES or NO in answer to the following questions. Consider the questions carefully, for they may well be the doorway to your deliverance from occult subjection and oppression if you have ever participated in or practiced these things. If there are multiple items in one question, underline the ones that apply to you.

YES   NO

____   ____   Have you ever visited a fortuneteller who told your fortune by the use of cards, tea leaves, palm reading, etc?

____   ____   Do you read or follow the horoscope?

____   ____   Has anyone ever hypnotized you?

____   ____   Have you ever practiced yoga or done exercises related to yoga?

____   ____   Have you ever attended a seance or spiritualist meeting at any time?

____   ____   Have you ever had a life or reincarnate reading'?

YES   NO

____   ____   Have you consulted ouiji board, or other fortune telling methods?

____   ____   Have you played with the so-called 'games' of an occult nature? (ESP, Telepathy, Kabala, Dungeons & Dragons, etc.)

____   ____   Have you ever consulted a medium?

____   ____   Have you ever sought healing through magic conjuration and charming, or through a Spiritualist, Christian Scientist, or anyone who practices 'spirit healing' psychic healing, hypnosis, metaphysical healing, use of the pendulum or trance for diagnosis, or any other occult means?

____   ____   Have you been to a chiropractor who treats through the use of ying and yang, the universal life forces in the spine?

____   ____   Have you ever sought to locate missing objects or persons by consulting someone who has psychic, clairvoyant, second sight, or psychometric powers?

____   ____   Have you practiced table-lifting, levitation, or automatic writing?

____   ____   Have you ever been given or worn an amulet, talisman or charm for luck or protection?

____   ____   Have you, or has anyone for you, practiced water witching using a twig or pendulum?

____   ____   Do you read or possess occult or spiritualist literature, e.g., books on astrology, interpretation of dreams, metaphysics, religious cults, self-realization, fortune telling, magic, ESP, clairvoyance, psychic phenomena?

____   ____   Do you ever call the Psychic Hotlines or access psychic advice on the computer?

____   ____   Do you often have nightmares or frightening dreams? Have you ever been "guided" by a dream?

____   ____   Have you experimented with or practiced ESP or telepathy? Have you ever "thought" at a person or tried to make them call or write you by your thoughts?

____   ____   Have you ever practiced any form of magic charming or ritual?

____   ____   Do you possess any occult or pagan religious objects, relics, or artifacts which may have been used in pagan temples and religious rites, or in the practice of sorcery, magic, divination, or spiritualism?

YES   NO

____   ____   Have you ever had your handwriting analyzed, practiced mental suggestion, cast a magic spell, or sought psychic experience?

____   ____   Have you ever listened to hard rock music for long periods of time? Do you have a strong identification with a musician (dead or alive)?

____   ____   Do you have strong identification with a movie star (dead or alive), actor/actress, or famous figure?

____   ____   Have you ever belonged to the Masons, DeMolay, Job's Daughters?

____   ____   Have you been involved in a lodge or organization requiring rituals for membership?

____   ____   Do you see auras?

____   ____   Do you ever 'feel' an evil presence?

____   ____   Have you ever been visited by a demon or an evil spirit?

____   ____   Have you ever gone in any temple or building that was not Christian (Buddhist temple, Mormon temple, Masonic temple, etc.)?

____   ____   Do you ever have very strong feelings of rage, a desire to commit suicide, murder, etc.?

____   ____   Have you ever been involved in any group involved in rebellion or terrorism?

____   ____   Have you had negative things or curses spoken over you?

____   ____   Have you been involved in satan worship?

____   ____   Have you ever practiced astral projection?

____   ____   Have you been involved in white magic: doing good things through the control of psychic and supernatural power?

____   ____   Have you been involved in black magic: psychic control through curses, use of the black arts, or any demon power for the purpose of harm?

____   ____   Have you had dreams with candles, hooded figures, or snakes?

____   ____   Do you have difficulty taking communion?

YES   NO

____   ____   Have you ever heard voices?

____   ____   Are you regularly awakened between the hours of 12:00 midnight and 3:00a.m.?

____   ____   Have you made any blood pacts?

____   ____   Have you ever felt you have participated in an immoral act with a demon?

____   ____   Have you suddenly had a feeling that you wanted to commit suicide?

____   ____   Have you ever had pains which seem to move and for which there is no medical cause?

____   ____   Have you ever wanted to cut yourself or have you ever intentionally cut yourself?

____   ____   Have you ever participated in a seance?

____   ____   Have you ever attended a New Age seminar?

____   ____   Have you had spiritual experiences that would be considered out of the ordinary?

____   ____   To your knowledge have any of your parents, grandparents, or great grandparents ever been involved in any occult, cultic, or non-Christian religious practices?

Have you ever been involved or attended any of the Eastern religions?

____Hinduism	____Buddhism
____Moslem	____Shintoism
____Bahai	____Rosicrucian
____Transcendental Meditation	____Zen Buddhism
____Hare Krishna	____Meher Baba
____The Riddle of Reincarnation	____Other
____Dhagwan Shree Rajneesh	

Have your ever been involved in or attended meetings conducted by modern cults, such as:

____Theosophy	____Mormons
____The Way	____Unitarian
____Children of God	____Eckankar
____Christian Science	____Worldwide Church of God
____Jehovah's Witnesses	____Unity
____Silva Mind Control	____E.S.T.
____Unification Church	____Scientology
	____Other

Ministry / Availability

In order to help us best match up a team with you we need to know the three best times of ministry for you.

Monday	am_____	pm_____
Tuesday	am_____	pm_____
Wednesday	am_____	pm_____
Thursday	am_____	pm_____
Friday	am_____	pm_____

Write a short summary of where you are right now and what you see as the problem in your life.

_____

_____

_____

_____

_____

_____

_____

_____

_____

Learning to Do What Jesus Did

Appendix H: Release Agreement for Prayer Recipient

Release Agreement

This ministry is called PRAYER MINISTRY. It is not professional counseling. We are not professional counselors and are not licensed or insured as such. We work with you only as you choose to work with us. We do not charge for our services.

God has seen fit to work with and through us in moving people toward wholeness. It is, therefore, our expectation that He will use us to help you, but we cannot promise results. We can only promise that we will do our best to work with God for your good and God's glory.

What usually happens in this type of ministry is that God brings another degree of healing in each session. There is a move toward wholeness as we seek healing together. Seldom is this all that is necessary for a person to attain the complete freedom he/she and God desire. Often it is advisable for the person to receive help from a professional counselor as well. It is also always advisable for the person to actively pursue spiritual disciplines such as church attendance, prayer, Bible study and worship along with the ministry.

We are committed to keep confidential whatever you share with us. We are, however, required by law to report to appropriate persons two kinds of things:

1. Any intent of a person to take harmful, dangerous, or criminal action against another person or against him/herself.

2. Any act of child or elderly abuse or neglect.

If it appears that such notification needs to be given, that intention will be shared with you first.

In summary, we would like you to do the following things:

1. Understand and agree to the above.

2. Be expectant, but not get upset or angry if all that you expect does not happen quickly.

3. Be patient with yourself, with us and with God.

4. Be prayerful and open for growth and change under the guidance of the Holy Spirit.

5. Engage your will to work with the Holy Spirit and us to move toward what God wants for you.

6. Forgive us if we make mistakes, forgive yourself if you make mistakes, and release God if He doesn't do things the way you expect them to be done.

Release of Liabilities

I, hereby release Wholeness Ministries, their Board of Directors, staff members, pastors, task force and lay ministers from all personal and corporate liability or responsibility for any present or future claims from myself, my heirs or assigns.

I further release them from all liability for any personal or psychological injury and, hereby, give my permission to review, consult, and advise per their discretion.

I release them from liability and responsibility in relation to the disclosure of information (only as required by law) of a personal and confidential nature, now and in the future.

Signature: _____ Date: _____

Witness: _____ Date: _____

Witness: _____ Date: _____

Appendix I: Deliverance Prayer Model

The following prayer is a model we often use to begin a deliverance session, especially when praying for a large group. This model was developed by Christian Healing Ministries, Jacksonville FL, USA.

THE DELIVERANCE PRAYER

In the Name of Jesus Christ and by the power of His cross and Blood and by the power of the Holy Spirit, I lift to the Lord myself, my family, our home, work place and each person for whom I am now praying. By the authority of the Word of God it is written "Whatsoever is bound on earth is bound in heaven; what is loosed on earth is loosed in heaven" (Matt. 18:18). Standing on the word of God and in the name of Jesus Christ I bind you Satan and all your evil spirits, demonic forces, satanic powers, principalities and forces of the air, water, fire, ground, the netherworld and the satanic forces of nature. I bind all evil interplay out of and away from each and every individual's spirit, mind and body for whom I am now praying and send these evil forces to the feet of Jesus Christ. Your assignments in the lives of these people are now broken.

In the Name of Jesus Christ I loose the **Holy Spirit** and the heavenly hosts to surround and protect each area and individual, and to seek out and cleanse with God's holy light all areas vacated by the forces of evil. I loose the Holy Spirit to permeate their spirit, mind and body, creating a hunger and thirst for God's Word to the glory of God the Father, the Son and Holy Spirit.

In the Name of Jesus Christ and by the power of His Word, I bind all spiritual, physical and mental rebellion, defiance, guilt, denial, deception, violence, confusion, fear of failure, procrastination, spirit of control, criticism, poverty, infirmity, self hatred, incest, anger, fear, anxiety, rejection, poor self-image, distrust, timidity, false pride, laziness, lethargy, need to control, and any occult spirit of darkness and death, in each of the people I am praying for, and I send these spirits to the feet of Jesus Christ, now. I loose the Spirit of obedience, love, peace, joy, acceptance, good self-image, discipline, relinquishment, freedom of guilt, a sound mind, truth, acceptance of self, trust, self-control, faithfulness, goodness, kindness, and the light and life of Jesus Christ in them.

I rebuke all spells, hexes, curses, voodoo practices, witchcraft, satanic rituals and prayers not of the Lord that have been sent our way and send them to Jesus Christ to deal with.

In the Name of Jesus Christ and by the power of His word, I take the Sword of the Spirit and cut every person free, for whom I am now praying, from all generational inherited sins, weaknesses, character defects, personality traits, and cellular and genetic disorders. I cut all bonds that are not of the Lord between us, our parents, our siblings, our children, and our grandparents.

In the Name of Jesus Christ we are now free to become the child of God the Lord intended us to be filled with love, peace, joy, patience, kindness, goodness, faithfulness and self-control. Thank you Lord, that you would grant all of us "according to the riches of your glory to be strengthened with power through your Holy Spirit in our inner being, so that Christ may dwell in our hearts, through faith, and that we being rooted and grounded in love, may be able to comprehend with all the saints what is the breadth, and length and height and depth and to know the love of Christ which surpasses knowledge, that we may be filled up to all the fullness of God" (Eph. 3:14-19).

Appendix J: Names of God

Those who know Your name will trust in You, For You, Lord, have never forsaken those who seek You. Psalm 9:10 (NIV)

Name	Meaning
Adonai	Lord, Master
El Elyon	The Most High God
El Gmolah	Lord God of Recompenses
El Olam	The Everlasting God
El Roi	Strong One Who Sees
El Shaddai	The All-Sufficient One
Elohim	Creator
Jehovah-hoseenu	The Lord Our Maker
Jehovah-jireh	The Lord Will Provide
Jehovah-mekoddishkem	The Lord Who Sanctifies You
Jehovah-nissi	The Lord My Banner
Jehovah-nakeh	The Lord That Smiteth
Jehovah-raah	The Lord My Shepherd
Jehovah-rapha	The Lord That Healeth
Jehovah-sabaoth	The Lord of Hosts
Jehovah-shalom	The Lord Is Peace
Jehovah-shammah	The Lord Is There
Jehovah-tsidkenu	The Lord Our Righteousness
Qanna	Jealous
Yahweh	Lord (Jehovah)

Appendix K: Frequently Asked Questions

Introduction

You will Always Have Questions

This appendix has been adapted from teaching material used at "Healing 87", a seminar presented by the Vineyard Christian Fellowship in Anaheim, CA. The seminar was conducted by John Wimber and Francis MacNutt

It is natural for questions to arise as an individual continues to move toward a ministry which includes praying regularly for the sick. Often questions can even keep a person from starting to pray for healing. At times unanswered questions can immobilize a person with fear. Questions must be faced and answered directly. An individual who genuinely wants answers to questions relating to healing has nothing to fear from a careful study of the scriptures. In this section, eight of the most commonly raised "problem teachings and problem texts" are clearly discussed. A thorough understanding of how these can be dealt with from a Biblical perspective will greatly enhance a person's confidence that healing is indeed a vitally important part of a Christian's life.

Scriptural Answers for Commonly Asked Questions

Does Everyone Get Healed?

- Jesus healed all who came to Him (Matthew 4:24, 8:16; Mark 1:32; Luke 6:18,19).

- There were obviously special times of anointing; "the power of the Lord was present to heal" (Luke 5:17). Note also Peter's shadow and Paul's handkerchiefs where all were healed (Acts 5:15, 16; 19: 11,12).

- However, Jesus healed only one man, not all, at the pool of Bethesda, a type of "hospital" (John 5:1-20). His explanation in the context is that He only does what He sees the Father doing.

- When the crowds came to be healed, Jesus would often withdraw privately for prayer. Why? (Luke 5:15,16).

- Therefore, not all are healed, although our desire is for all to be healed.

Does Every Healing Happen Immediately?

- Most of the healings recorded in the New Testament happened "immediately" (e.g. Mark 31,42).

- Jesus had to pray twice for a blind man after he saw men like trees walking about (Mark 8:28).

- Sometimes physical healings are progressive because emotional and other needs must first be met (3 John 2).

What About the Use of Medicine?

- 2 Chronicles 16:12- Asa sought a physician in his sickness and not the Lord. This does not mean that one should not go to a doctor. 'Physicians' in those days used occult practices.

- Timothy was encouraged to use a little wine for his stomach because of its medicinal benefits (1 Timothy 5:23).

- Oil and spittle were regarded as having healing qualities and were used by Jesus and His disciples in their healings (John 9:6; Mark 7:33, 8:23, 6:13). Whether these elements possessed healing qualities or not, is not the issue. The fact is that Jesus did not avoid association with medicine, in fact, He seemed to sanction it.

- Therefore, it is not wrong to use medicine. God is the source of healing, but He uses various means.

What About Dying?

- We must accept that there is a time to die; it is appointed unto man once to die (Ecclesiastes 3:2, Hebrews 9:27).

- You cannot control the time when God takes you. However, you do not have to die before your time through sin, sickness, and judgment (1 Corinthians 11:30).

- Sickness does not have to be the cause of death, and even then, Jesus has control over death and can raise the dead (e.g. when Jesus heard of Lazarus' illness He said it would not result in death and stayed two extra days where He was. Four days after the death, Jesus raised Lazarus to life - John 11:1-6).

- Therefore, we need to be aware when a sickness is "unto death" and minister comfort and courage to the dying.

Is Sickness Always Caused by Sin?

- The blind man in John 9 did not have the problem because he or his parents sinned, but so that the works of God might be manifested in him.

- The pool of Bethesda experience teaches that lameness came through sin in the case of the man Jesus healed (John 5:14).

- The Old Testament teaches a direct relationship between sin and sickness (Deuteronomy 28:15,21), whereas the New Testament teaches Jesus' healing power over the works of the devil (Acts 10:38).

- Therefore, although sickness comes ultimately because of the curse of sin, not all sickness is caused by specific sins.

What About Believers Who Do Not Get Well?

- Paul had an affliction, the reason for which is not cited (Galatians 4:13-16).

- Trophimus was left sick at Miletus with no real explanation. (2 Timothy 4:20).

- Epaphroditus was ill and almost died, but God had mercy (Philippians 2:26,27).

- Timothy had a persistent stomach weakness. Paul prescribed some wine (1 Timothy 5:2).

- Some areas could be checked in the case of people not being healed—such as sin, unforgiveness, emotional needs, unbelief or faithlessness—or just to leave it with God.

Are Suffering and Sickness From God?

- Sickness and suffering in the Christian life are not synonymous. There is no indication in scripture that suffering means or includes sickness. Christ was never sick, but He suffered persecution. (See Acts 10:38; Philippians 1:29).

- It is God's nature to heal, not to "teach" us through sickness. Sickness is generally not beneficial (e.g. the lame man in John 5 made a friend of his sickness and was robbed for 38 years).

- If we are drawn nearer to God because of sickness, the virtue lies in God's goodness which leads us to repentance and acceptance, rather than in what the sickness has done (Romans 2:4; cf. 1 Corinthians 11:29-32).

- "Unnecessary suffering" in innocent children and helpless people cannot be blamed on "God, Who is Love". The curse of sin in the world results in constant war, famine, need, etc; and sometimes the affect of the sins of the parents are present in the bloodline of the family to the third and fourth generation (Psalms 55:5; Exodus 34:6,7; John 10:10).

What the New Testament Teaches

- Sickness is the result of the work of the devil and his kingdom.

- All sickness ultimately comes from sin (the fall); but not all cases of sickness come as a result of specific, personal sin.

- Healing is the manifestation of the Kingdom of God and takes place among those receptive.

- Healing flows in and through the community of the Kingdom, bringing social well-being.

Appendix L: Guidelines for Prayer Teams in Group Settings

The purpose of a Ministry Team is to facilitate the move of the Holy Spirit. You are there as instruments to release God's love, healing and empowering to those who indicate a desire for prayer; to bless, edify, and comfort; to minister in the style of Jesus. To minister simply means to serve, to give of yourself. We ask you to submit yourself to the leadership, style, "flavor" and general purpose of the meetings you are in, which may mean laying aside some of your own ministry "techniques." We need to all flow in unity with one heart so the Lord can do what He wants to do in the manner He wants to do it.

IT IS IMPORTANT to remember that in this setting being a team member does not give you license to rebuke, correct or give direction for someone's life. It does not provide an opportunity for in-depth ministry involvement, (i.e. Inner Healing, Counseling, or Deliverance), although we find that the Holy Spirit himself frequently brings about these results sovereignly. Generally we are not trained as counselors; we are there to pray and that is what we should be spending the majority of our time doing.

Being on a team is not a "life membership." You may be asked to step aside for a season of personal renewal. It is important that each team member regularly receive the Holy Spirit's refreshing so that ministry will come from the "overflow" of His life in you.

1. When praying for individuals, **always pray in teams of at least two**. Keep your eyes open and watch closely what the Spirit is doing. Some of the manifestations you may see are as follows:

    • The individual may begin to tremble slightly

    • The eyelids may begin to flutter rapidly

    • Sometimes the face will flush or they will break out in a sweat as if they are suddenly very warm.

    These are all visible signs of the presence of the Holy Spirit and are very normal. If no manifestations of the Holy Spirit come within a few minutes, it is often wise to simply ask them, "What are you feeling or sensing?" If they are sensing or feeling something continue to pray for them. If they are feeling or sensing nothing then you can continue to pray for them or you can say something like, "I want you to enjoy the presence of the Lord, to worship Him and soak in His anointing for a little while. Someone will come and pray with you again a little later on."

    You never want to make a person feel that they are unable to receive or are resisting the Holy Spirit just because they are not openly manifesting something. We are called to encourage and love, not speak words that will bring rejection or discouragement. Other team members will pray for them, or you can come back when you have finished ministering to several others.

2. Do not force ministry! If the Spirit is not doing something, relax and remember that there will always be another opportunity. Trusting the Word of Wisdom is essential, that is, knowing when He is doing something personal within an individual and not interrupting that special "conversation."

   Also, if you are "blank" or not receiving anything, get another Ministry Team Member to take over for you and move on.

3. If the person continues to have a hard time receiving you might help them in the following ways:

   • Help them deal with a tendency to rationalize. Calm their fears in regards to losing control. Assure them that the Holy Spirit will treat them with the utmost love.

   • Let them know what to expect - that even when the Holy Spirit is blessing them, they will have a clear mind and can usually stop the process at any point if they desire.

   • The Holy Spirit often moves in what are described as "waves" similar to the blowing wind.

   • If they are praying along with you, encourage them to "be still and know that God is God" and stay focused on the Lord. He loves them intensely and longs for them to know Him intimately.

4. Generally it is helpful to have people stand to receive ministry. This seems to allow the Holy Spirit more freedom to move at the beginning. In consideration, for assurance of safety and comfort, have a ministry assistant stand behind the person receiving ministry to catch them if they "rest" in the Spirit. Some people have a "fear of falling" and hurting themselves. Help them to sit down, kneel or "rest" carefully, especially if they have back problems, are pregnant or elderly.

5. When people "rest in the Spirit" keep praying for them. It seems best to pray and "soak" the person for a couple of minutes. It is best not to touch them while praying as this can be distracting. Especially no massaging or caressing. Also, some want to get up far too quickly. Encourage them to just relax and enjoy what God is doing. God often works powerfully when one is down on the floor. Sometimes it will be noticeable and other times it might be quiet and inward. Often, allowing people to get up too quickly seems to work against what the Lord wants to do.

6. After a period of time you may move on to minister to others that are waiting for ministry and occasionally return to the first one to see how they are doing. Many feel very vulnerable while in this position and appreciate the loving care given by faithful team members. Also, they need to be guarded from others bumping into them while they are on the floor and/or making uncalled for comments within their hearing.

7. **ABSOLUTELY!** be very careful not to push people over in your zeal! This is offensive and will cause people to grow resistant to the real manifestation. Sometimes it is wise to not even touch them. Watch over-enthusiasm and a tendency to want to "help God Out", especially when you are sensing a strong anointing within you or if you are tired and getting a little impatient. If this happens withdraw your hand from the person immediately and as soon as possible withdraw and get some rest.

8. When you are praying there is at times a "backwash phenomena". This happens when the presence of the spirit is very strong and the anointing begins to make you feel weak. If necessary, sit for a few minutes until you feel strong enough to stand and minister again. If your hand or body is shaking and you feel this may be a distraction, pray with your hands slightly away from the person. If a stronger manifestation begins to happen within you and you are feeling very weak, withdraw from ministering for awhile and let the Lord bless you.

9. We pray in the style of "laying on of hands-not leaning on of hands". Give a light touch only and watch heavy pressure - generally on the forehead, top of head, shoulder, or hands. No inappropriate touching(i.e. do not touch a woman's chest, abdomen, legs, etc.) It is distracting to rub, massage or caress. This is inappropriate and can be quite distracting.

   It is best to have men pray with men, women with women or a man/woman team praying with either sex.

10. If the individual you are praying with begins to scream or cry in a loud disrupting manner, causing a significant distraction or drawing attention to themselves, it is best to quiet them down by taking control and removing them from the room. Sometimes when this screaming or crying happens it is difficult to discern whether it is of God, of the flesh, or demonic. If it is of God and you "shut it down" and take them to another room, He is quite capable of continuing to minister in spite of your mistakes. If it is of the flesh or demonic you definitely want to "shut it down" and minister in another place or set up a time to continue ministry in another setting.

    There are few "emergencies" in the Kingdom of God, and you most definitely want to pray for deliverance ministry on your terms, not when the demonic happens to cork off. If this seems rather harsh to you please remember that in most cases the demonic has been there for many years and waiting a few more hours or days is not going to make much of a difference. This distraction can also happen with laughter that sounds like or turns into something which sounds like cackling or mockery. This must also be shut down.

11. If you are receiving a "Word of Knowledge," pray prayers related to those words. If you are not sure how to begin you can say something like, "I sense the Lord may be saying... Does this mean anything to you?" Let the majority of prophetic words for encouragement, edification, exhortation or comfort flow from prayer ministry."

12. You will seldom err if you pray Biblical prayers such as:

    * Come Holy Spirit

    * Let your kingdom come Lord, on earth as it is in Heaven

    * A release for a deeper revelation of the Father's love

    * Anointing for service

    * Release of the gifts and callings

    * Bring the light and expel the darkness

    * Open the eyes of their understanding to know the magnitude of the gift of Salvation

    * "More, Lord" How much more will the Father give to those who ask...

    * Peace... ruling and reigning in their hearts

13. Don't project what God has been doing with you onto the person you are praying with. For example, if you have been laughing, crying, resting, or any one of a number of other manifestations, don't pressure them to do the same. Find out what God is doing for them and bless it.

14. If you are drawn to pray in your spiritual language while ministering to someone, it is best to pray very quietly so as to not distract or even offend. They may not understand what you are doing or be afraid of it. Besides, this is a conversation between you and God and does not need to be heard by others. If you are drawn to pray in tongues while ministering to someone, follow through by giving the interpretation so the person can be blessed (1 Corinthians 14:6).

    Some recipients habitually pray aloud while receiving ministry. Encourage them to be quiet and just receive - it is difficult to drink in and pour out at the same time.

15. The person you are praying with needs to be assured that they are the most important one for that moment. Avoid the tendency to let your mind and eyes wander onto other things or other people or other situations in the room. Don't become distracted with other issues or manifestations in the room. You may find it helpful to close your eyes and re-focus at this point.

16. Finally, as a member of a prayer team, you own appearance and personal hygiene are essential. Use breath mints and deodorant. Do not chew gum or suck on candies. Have clean

hands and hair. Wear clean and appropriate clothing. Do not user strong scented perfume, cologne, hand lotion or after-shave lotion; if you are unsure about how much scent is enough then don't use any. Nothing about you should distract from what God is doing.

Guidelines For Catching People

1. Please do not push or pull anyone over. This will ultimately backfire, and could physically injure the person or others.

2. Do not hold anyone up by grabbing their shoulders or upper back.

3. When laying hands on people, do just that. Do not rub or do other things that might be annoying.

4. When preparing to catch someone, keep your elbows close to your sides and put your hands at the small of their back. This gives people confidence that you are behind them and does not interfere with the prayer process.

   Attempt to move back with the person as they fall rather than trying to take their whole weight upon yourself. Lower yourself by bending at the knees, not at the waist.

5. Assisting in this role is a vital part of ministry so please concentrate on being a helper, being right there when you are needed, not gazing around the room and/or visiting with others nearby. It is very disconcerting for the prayer minister when they realize you are not there in a crucial moment, and someone could be injured when the person falls and you are not ready.

   If you become tired or it's time for your own ministry, then tell your leader so someone else can be asked to assist.

6. This time of being a ministry assistant can be a valuable one for you to listen and learn and quietly intercede for the individual receiving prayer These guidelines were adapted from some excellent material prepared by the Toronto Airport Christian Fellowship. Minor changes have been made to adapt to the local setting.

Appendix M: Building and Training a Healing Prayer Team

1. Examine your own commitment to healing and training others to heal the sick.

   A. It's important to consider the following key questions before you move into prayer team ministry.

      1. Are we called to pray for the sick? (Mt. 10:1,7-8; 28:18-19.)

      2. Are we willing to be obedient to this call?

      3. Are we ready to pay the price of doing the work of healing the sick?

         a. There will be suffering.

         b. There will be rejection.

         c. There will be fierce opposition from Satan.

   B. Pray for God to send around you some others with the same desire and vision for prayer team ministry. As these others come, renew your commitment as a team to personal growth in your relationship to God by doing the following:

      1. Taking a fresh look at your whole life and its conformity to Christ (Romans 8:29;12:2). Where there needs to be repentance, do it!

         a. Allow God to show you those things in your life that do not conform to the image of Jesus.

         b. Allow God to transform you by the renewing of your mind.

      2. Scriptures tell us to "seek the Kingdom of God and His righteousness" (Mt. 6:33). Examine your own life and deal with those "things" that stand in the way of putting God's kingdom first in your life.

         a. Worship, pray, and read the Scriptures daily.

         b. Receive a fresh outpouring of the Spirit yourselves—NO SUBSTITUTE—you cannot give what you do not have!!

3. "Walk in the Spirit" daily.

   a. Learn afresh to "hear" and obey the Spirit by spending time listening for His voice.

   b. Be open to receive all the gifts of the Spirit and begin moving in the supernatural on a daily basis.

   c. Expect God to speak and move, giving you dreams and vision, words and direction, signs and wonders—and He will!!

II. Get personal training in healing the sick in Jesus' name from those who are already doing it with success.

   A. Practice in actually doing prayer for healing.

      1. Watch others pray.

      2. Do the prayer ministry work along side of them.

      3. Listen to the Spirit as you observe and pray.

   B. Learn all you can about the prayer and healing ministry.

      1. Attend training sessions.

      2. Ask questions and get answers you need.

      3. Read Scriptures daily, especially the Gospels.

      4. Study excellent books on healing:

         a. Francis MacNutt: <u>Healing</u> and <u>The Power to Heal</u>

         b. David Seamands: <u>Healing for Damaged Emotions</u>

         c. J.S. Baxter: <u>Divine Healing of The Body</u>

         d. John Wimber: <u>Power Healing</u> and <u>Power Evangelism</u>

         e. Bill Johnson: <u>When Heaven Invades Earth</u>

C. Study the model for healing prayer used by Wholeness Ministries.

    1.   It is considerably different from either Pentecostal or Sacramental models.

    2.   What are the Key Characteristics of this model?

        a. Naturalness/non-theatrics/healing is normative

        b. Integrity/strong emphasis on the needs of and care for the subject

        c. Open to the whole body

        d. Listening to the Spirit and being directed by Him

III. Begin doing the prayer ministry yourself in your own fellowship.

A. Begin teaching about Biblical healing.

    1.   Clearly and thoroughly teach the Scriptures.

    2.   Teach the basic principles.

B. Begin praying for the sick regularly in a normal, public gathering.

    1.   Use a major weekly gathering; Sunday morning.

    2.   Pray for healing daily in your office, hospitals, and homes.

C. Refine and clarify the model of healing prayer for your fellowship through continual, personal practice.

D. Show the people how to pray for healing on a regular basis.

    1.   Demonstrate.

    2.   Explain.

E. Give many opportunities for testimonies of those who are miraculously healed by God.

IV. Begin training those who are responsive to what you are doing.

A. Begin training classes or seminars using materials you develop or those available through Wholeness Ministries.

    1.   Overview the healings which took place in both the Old and New Testaments.

2.   Study the different settings, teachings and practices of Jesus in the Gospels.

3.   Study the Apostles' and early church's healing practices in the Gospels and Acts.

4.   Study the teaching models from the Pentecostal, Charismatic and liturgical groups that are experiencing healing.

B. Both "demonstrate" and "explain" in all training settings, how to pray for healing so that there is always an emphasis on doing the healing ministry.

C. Pray for the Holy Spirit to come in power upon your trainees.

1.   Lay hands on them for empowering by the Spirit and releasing of all the gifts.

2.   Get them into actually doing the ministry.

D. Use "On the Job" training from the beginning.

1.   Model the practices yourself and let them watch.

2.   Continue to pray for healing ,and let them do it with you.

3.   Let them take the lead and you help, encourage and counsel them.

4.   Release them to do the praying as you observe and give them feedback.

E. Continue using the trainees regularly in praying for healing during your church gatherings, letting them function more and more freely.

F. Encourage them to function in prayer ministry in small home groups.

V. Be aware of key leaders who will emerge.

A. Take special note of the following:

1.   Especially anointed and gifted persons

2.   Those who are teachable and regularly put into use what they are being taught

3.   Spiritually mature persons; those with a lifestyle that demonstrates what they believe

4.   Those ready to give significant time (faithful and available)

5.   Those who relate well to others (outgoing)

B. Pray and watch for those whom God will send your way that you can bring around you as a "Task Force" to help with oversight and training others in prayer team ministry.

    1.   Spend personal time with these people building friendships with them and between them.

    2.   Begin using them visibly to aid you in prayer settings, to lead and facilitate the ministry, so they are seen as models along with you.

    3.   Ask them to begin making contacts with the prayer teams, caring for them and reporting to you as needed.

    4.   Meet with these leaders weekly to encourage them, pray for the prayer teams and evaluate the ministry.

    5.   Deploy your leaders into specific responsibilities of modeling, encouraging, trouble shooting, monitoring, teaching, caring for the team and reporting.

VI. Teach your prayer teams to deal graciously with those who oppose divine healing.

A. Encounters with hostile Christians who reject healing for today or who may disagree with your teaching will occur. Remember that dealing graciously with them is a definite part of the training process.

B. Key practices to use:

    1.   Don't grieve the Holy Spirit. Don't argue or fight with a Christian brother.

    2.   Let the Holy Spirit direct you. Expect a word from Him.

    3.   Be Christ-like with humble, kindly and gracious words and actions. (2 Tim. 2:24-26)

    4.   Answer concerns or objections from Scripture.

    5.   Depend on God to protect and vindicate you.

C. Model behavior before your team and encourage them to act the same way.

VII. Evaluate closely those who want to minister with you.

A. Take note of people who are...

    1.   Especially self-focused

    2.   Resistant to the model of healing prayer used in your fellowship.

3. Spiritually immature

4. People who are irregular

5. Contentious, arrogant, socially incapable people

6. People who give evidence of spiritual bondage or demonization

B. Understand that allowing such troubled people to function with the prayer teams will greatly hinder any healing or teamwork.

C. Discuss that person's conditions with your leadership and develop a loving course of remedial action: such as:

1. Correction and encouragement to remain on the team under supervision

2. Correction and redirection into another ministry

VIII. Care for your prayer teams.

A. Spend special time in prayer for and with them.

B. Be aware of the enemy's attack on the teams individually and corporately.

C. Debrief frequently and take special note of what God is doing and what needs are arising.

D. Correct any problems immediately; don't let them linger.

E. Look out for and warn your teams about :

1. Burnout

2. Friction between members

3. Strong attractions between members of opposite sex that seem to be leading toward moral failure

F. Have special times of retreat together for rest and relaxation.

G. Be especially sensitive to "emotional lows" after spiritually intense ministry sessions.

H. Make prayer for healing and the supernatural NORMAL![1]

Learning to Do What Jesus Did

Appendix N: Spiritual Warfare and Healing

I. Recognize that healings and demonstrations of the presence and power of God often (always) bring counter attack from Satan!

   A. Healing by God's power marks the clear advance of the Kingdom of God into the Kingdom of darkness.

      1.   Jesus' healings and demon expulsions -Mt. 12:22-28

      2.   Paul's preaching of the Kingdom demonstrated by extraordinary signs - Acts 19:8-11

   B. Healing often exposes the enemy.

      1.   Woman with crooked spine actually demon afflicted - Lk. 13:10-14

      2.   A dumb man is healed by having a demon cast out - Mt. 9:32,33

   C. Healing will, therefore, often be followed by counter-attack by the forces of darkness.

      1.   Mt. 8 - Three healings followed by two direct attacks!

      2.   Acts 14 - Signs and wonders twice followed by attempted murder

   D. It's vital to recognize that healing is a major battleground and that entering this ministry means a life of warfare!

II. Recognize that the enemy will have simple, specific and lethal objectives in mind when he brings his forces against you..

   A. Preliminary objectives:

      1.   To Kill you!

         a. Murderer from the beginning (John 8:44)

         b. Intends to destroy leaders of the Kingdom of God

      2.   To wound you - put you out of action, at least temporarily.

      3.   To make you sin and bring God's discipline down on you (Balaam/David/Ananias and Sapphira)

4.   To infest your life and that of the troops of God's army —he wants to infiltrate the ranks and dilute your ministry.

5.   To bring division among God's servants.

6.   To enable defection (Demas)

7.   To disorient the activities of the Kingdom - get energies flowing in useless activities.

B.   Ultimate goals:

1.   To drive out the Kingdom of God - cause retreat and to retake lost territory.

2.   To stop the advance of the Kingdom - to bring the warfare to a stand off.

3.   To at least slow the advance of God's Kingdom

4.   To hinder and hopefully stop all supernatural manifestations of the presence of God's Kingdom.

III. Recognize the enemy's principal tactics of war against your healing ministry.

A.   In the earliest stages of ministry, the enemy will do all he can to stimulate UNBELIEF IN DIVINE HEALING.

1.   His classic question "Did God say?" will be raised again and again.

2.   Another classic line of argument coming out of the darkness is "Divine healing is not for our day."

B.   Another tactic characteristic of the early days of supernatural ministry is the attempt to create SELF DOUBT OVER HEALING.

1.   The thought will come to mind: "Others can heal the sick, but I can't."

2.   Another related thought: "I don't have the gift of healing, so I won't see the sick healed."

C.   Once you have begun to see some healing that cannot be discounted, the enemy's tactics switch to FOCUS ONTO THOSE WHO AREN'T HEALED.

1.   The enemy will seek to play down fabulous healings of cancer and blindness together with consistent help given over less outstanding cures, while constantly bringing up the cases in which there was little or no visible effect of prayer.

2.   Initial and close relation cases of death are principal ways of driving sincere Christians out of the healing ministry.

3.   The enemy's line of argument is: "Since these persons were not healed, the others whom you thought were, really aren't healed either. Inability in some cases discounts all!"

4.   Warfare can become very intense at these points with the enemy doing all he can to break the back of the healing work and preserve His strongholds.

D.   DIRECT FRONTAL ATTACK THROUGH DEMON MANIFESTATIONS is a strategy that is intended to bowl you over and convince you that the enemy's power is greater than yours in Christ.

1.   Demon manifestation is the clearest expression of confrontation between the two kingdoms.

2.   Such power encounters will usually happen on the "enemy's turf" where he feels the highest potential of driving you back and creating doubts and discouragement. Wait and do it in the light if your can, not in the night.

3.   These encounters come most often at night and amid confusing or fearful circumstances.

E.   The enemy will also do all he can to bring forth UNBELIEVING, DISCOURAGING WORDS AND ATTITUDES from "friendly" sources.

1.   Jesus experienced this at Caeserea Philippi. The discouraging words of Peter were actually inspired by Satan (Mt. 16:22,23).

2.   Unbelieving friends can be significant channels of demonic disheartement.

F.   The enemy will be very attuned to times of WEARINESS.

1.   Elijah's time of greatest spiritual collapse came after his greatest victory of supernatural demonstration. After days of spiritual confrontation, earnest prayer, and great physical exertion, he lost his bearings amid total exhaustion, became afraid and ran.

G.   Attempts to BRING SICKNESS upon a healer or healing team are frequent. Nearly every team served on has battled sickness while healing the sick.

H.   BLINDSIDE ATTACKS are another frequent strategy of the enemy — introducing trouble suddenly from a totally unexpected source.

I. The enemy's oldest tools of temptation can be his most devastating:

    1.   Sexual immorality brought David into years of defeat and pain. How many great healing ministries were destroyed here?

    2.   Lust for money undid Ananias and Sapphira amid great supernatural events.

    3.   Stimulation of greatest area of weakness.

J. Every possible means will be used by the forces of darkness to SEPARATE BRETHREN! No matter what happens don't be separated.

K. The enemy will definitely attempt to use ACCIDENTS OF NATURE against the Kingdom's advance. Don't be presumptuous; you could die before your time.

    1.   Jesus met this in Mt. 8 when a storm seemed likely to take their lives at sea just before ministry in a new territory was to begin.

L. ATTACKS BY PEOPLE under demonic inspiration or control may also occur as the healing ministry progresses.

    1.   Jesus constantly met this:

      a. Mt. 8:28 Gadarene demoniacs

      b. Mt. 12:22 Pharisees accusations

      c. Lk. 4:28-30 Murdering attempt in Nazareth

      d. Jn. 10:31-39 Jews in Jerusalem

      e. John 19,20 Jewish leaders who killed Jesus

    2.   Apostles continual experience

      a. Acts 4,5 Arrested for preaching Christ

      b. Acts 7,8 Martyrdom of Stephen, persecution of church

      c. Acts 12 Martyrdom of James and arrest of Peter

      d. Acts 13 Resistance by Elymas

      e. Acts 14 Attempts to molest and murder Paul and Barnabas

IV. Recognize that you have powerful weapons at your disposal. If they are used wisely and consistently, you will win the warfare and advance the Kingdom.

    A. Realize you're in an all out war involving eternal life and death.

        1. You must learn to "see" what the Father is doing and consistently follow His lead. Jesus said, "I do only what I see the Father doing."

        2. You must discern enemy presence and action and take up arms to fend him off and drive him away.

    B. Stay close to Jesus Christ Himself.

        1. He is our model in warfare as well as ministry; He is our Captain and Protector.

        2. Be consistent in worship, devotion, prayer, scripture reading and in maintaining real relationship with Christ. Spend time on your face before the throne of God.

    C. Follow Jesus' commands consistently and daily.

        1. Heal the sick.

        2. Cleanse lepers.

        3. Expel demons.

        4. Raise the dead.

        5. Don't stop, no matter what!!

    D. Be ready for counter attack—Put on and keep on your armor.

        1. Do what is right (Breastplate).

        2. Speak the truth (Belt).

        3. Think on the things of the gospel (Helmet).

          a. Destroy argument against power of God (2 Cor. 10).

          b. Set your mind on things of Christ (Rom. 8; Phil. 4).

        4. Believe God — expect miracles.

5. Live in peace with others (Sandals). Don't get in the ring. Don't put on the gloves.

6. Keep on even in the face of the death of comrades.

7. Pray about everything.

    a. "Prayer is the battle." Go into the closet and fight the battle, and then go out into victory.

    b. You have not, because you ask not. When counter attack comes, FIGHT!

E. Do hand to hand combat with the enemy using sword and shield:

1. Fend off fiery missiles with determined faith.

2. Swing the Sword of the Spirit - cut the enemy with rebuke from God's Word! (Jesus with Peter).

F. Resist the devil and he will flee:

1. Resist temptation to sin - stand for right.

2. Resist division - be reconciled, stay close to the troops.

3. Resist extreme weariness - get rest.

4. Resist old family patterns - get prayer for breaking of old bondages.

5. Resist presumption - don't let the enemy drag you out into foolish vulnerability.

6. Resist discouragement by fixing your heart on God's promises.

    a. Do not lose heart (2 Cor. 4).

    b. Beware empty words.

G. Endure suffering like a good soldier of Jesus Christ (2 Tim. 1).

H. Don't stop healing the sick until you see Jesus' face![1]

Appendix O: Scheduling a Healing/Training Conference

What Does Wholeness Ministries Offer?

Our ministry of healing prayer is based upon the life and ministry of Jesus, believing that His mandate, given in Luke 4:18-19, is also the calling of the Church today. In order to equip His Body to pray for others under the guidance and power of the Holy Spirit we offer a three-fold ministry:

Teaching

We have developed this manual, which has proved to be an invaluable tool for instruction during conferences and continued training after a conference has ended. Conference workshops are available to cover each of the sections of the manual.

Wholeness Ministries can also provide in-depth teaching on a particular aspect of the healing ministry that is of special interest to your group.

Equipping

Our style of teaching helps each individual to see by demonstration and modeling how to pray for others. Most workshops include opportunities for attendees to participate in prayer ministry as either the recipient of prayer or as one of the prayer team members.

Conference attendees are also encouraged to participate, observe and ask questions during the opportunities for ministry in general sessions.

Healing

It is not uncommon during conferences to see healing occur on many levels - physical, spiritual, emotional, and psychological. Some people experience instant healing and others begin to experience an on-going process of healing.

A Wholeness Ministries conference provides a safe place where this healing, deliverance, growth and wholeness can begin.

What Happens at a Wholeness Ministries Conference?

Mike Evans and one or more team members usually conduct weekend conferences. Prayer Team Training Conferences are offered in Bakersfield, CA as often as demand indicates and can be scheduled in other locations upon request. The schedule can be tailored to the needs of your group. A typical weekend conference would include the following sessions.

Friday Evening

Registration and a General Session which includes praise and worship, a message or teaching and an opportunity for ministry.

Saturday Morning

A General Session that includes praise and worship and an overview of prayer team ministry followed by selected workshops.

Saturday Afternoon

Additional workshops.

Saturday Evening

A General Session that includes praise and worship, a message and an extended opportunity for ministry.

Sunday Morning

Mike Evans is available to participate in the morning worship service if that option is appropriate for your group.

Workshop Topics

Workshops include teaching and "hands-on" training in subjects such as these:

- Recruiting and Training Prayer Teams

- Ministry Organization

- Biblical Basis for a Healing Ministry

- The Role of Faith and Authority in Prayer

- How to Pray for Physical Healing

- Understanding and Praying for Inner Healing

- Forgiveness and Healing Prayer

- A Balanced Approach to Deliverance Ministry

- Essentials in Understanding Spiritual Warfare

Who is Mike Evans?

Mike Evans is the Founder and Director of Wholeness Ministries located in Bakersfield, California. Mike is a graduate of Golden Gate University and earned his Masters degree in Christian Education and was ordained in 1982. Mike was an associate pastor from 1976 to 1994 at Bakersfield Christian Life Center. In 1989 Mike founded Wholeness Ministries, a ministry whose purpose is to train and equip believers to minister to those in need of physical, spiritual or emotional healing. Mike and his team have ministered healing in Canada, Northern Ireland, England, Puerto Rico, Hungary, India and extensively throughout the United States.

Comments from Churches Who Held a Conference

"Mike's ministry was superb; there was evidence of a deep spirituality there. The seeds that were sown today will grow and blossom in our congregations and spill over into our Province which needs to know about wholeness!" Rev. Isaac Thompson, Committee on Divine Healing; Belfast, N. Ireland

"Your style and manner, plus your personal experience with Christ, have opened our eyes to wonderful possibilities in the Lord as we continue to explore the challenge before us in prayer team ministry." Rev. Victor M. Vazquez; First Baptist Church; Juncos, Puerto Rico

"Our church has been blessed by Mike Evans' teaching and training on the healing ministry. Mike is compassionate, gifted by God, experienced in building and guiding prayer teams for the local church and in practical hands-on 'how-tos' in healing. His teaching gave us the jump start that we needed. I commend him to you enthusiastically." Don Williams; Coast Vineyard; LaJolla, California

Our purpose in creating this manual is to help people know the healing love of God. We would like to reach as many people as possible who need God's healing touch by providing this training manual.

If this manual has helped you and you wish to share a copy with a friend, we would like to make additional copies available to you. Please complete the order form below. You may also use the form if you want to be added to our monthly newsletter mailing list.

When completed, send this form to:
Wholeness Ministries
P.O. Box 80503
Bakersfield, CA 93380
(661) 833-2920
www.wholeness.org

Name _____

Address _____

_____

City _____

State, Zip, Country _____

Phone (_____)_____

Number of manuals _____ $18.95 each _____

California residents, add 7.25% sales tax _____

Shipping (from table below) _____

Donation to Wholeness Ministries _____

Total amount enclosed _____

[ ] Please add me to your monthly newsletter mailing list.

U.S. Shipping Rates*	
To separate addresses	$4.00 each
To the same address	$4.00 for the first manual $2.50 for each additional manual

Enclose specific shipping instructions if ordering manuals to be shipped to other addresses

* Please call for shipping rates to addresses outside the U.S.

Appendix Q: Endnotes

Section 2: The Role of Faith and Authority

1. Francis MacNutt, <u>Healing</u>, (New York: Image Books, 1990) pp. 117-119.
2. Adapted from Dr. Charles Kraft, <u>I Give You Authority</u>-Kraft (Chosen Books, 1997) p67
3. Ibid, p.68

Section 3: Introduction to Physical Healing

1. This material, "The Power of the Testimony," was adapted from a teaching given by Bill Johnson, Bethel Church, Redding, Ca. 2003.
2. Kris Vallotton, A Call To War, (Bethel Church, 2002) pp.60

Section 4: Repentance

1. Francis Frangipane, <u>The Three Battlegrounds</u>, (N.P., Advancing Church Publications, 1989) p.4.
2. Cindy Jacobs, <u>Possessing the Gates of the Enemy</u>, (Tarrytown, N.Y.: Chosen Books, 1991) p 43.
3. Francis Frangipane, <u>The Three Battlegrounds</u>, (N.P., Advancing Church Publications, 1989) p. 8.
4. Ibid., p.8

Section 5: Inner Healing and Forgiveness

1. John Wimber, <u>Signs and Wonders and Church Growth</u>, (Anaheim: VMI, 1987) p. 3.
2. Francis MacNutt, <u>Healing</u>, (Altamonte Springs: Creation House, 1988) pp. 185-187
3. Charles H. Kraft, <u>Defeating Dark Angels</u>, (Ann Arbor, Michigan: Servant Publications, 1992) p. 142.
4. J. Sidlow Baxter, Untitled Sermon, (Bakersfield, CA: Bakersfield Christian Life Center, March 28, 1988.)
5. Jack W. Hayford, <u>The Power and the Blessing</u>, (N.P., Victor Books, 1994) p. 48.
6. Gary Smalley and John Trent, <u>The Blessing</u>, (Thomas Nelson Publishing, 1986) p. 144.
7. David A. Seamands and Beth Funk, <u>Healing for Damaged Emotions Workbook</u>, (N.P.: Victor Books, 1992) p.132
8. Neil Anderson, <u>Freedom in Christ Conference Handbook</u>, January 24-27, 1995, (Anaheim, Vineyard Ministries International, 1995) p. 106.
9. Charles H. Kraft, <u>Defeating Dark Angels</u>, (Ann Arbor, Michigan: Servant Publications, 1992) p. 149.
10. We are greatly indebted to Charles Kraft for his material on emotions in <u>Deep Wounds, Deep Healing</u>, (Ann Arbor, MI, Servant Publications, 1993) pp. 184-187.

Section: 6 Deliverance

1. Charles H. Kraft, <u>Deep Wounds, Deep Healing</u>, (Ann Arbor, MI, Servant Publications, 1993) p. 260.
2. Francis MacNutt, <u>Deliverance from Evil Spirits</u>, (Grand Rapids: Chosen Books, 1995) p. 158.
3. Charles H. Kraft, <u>Deep Wounds, Deep Healing</u>, (Ann Arbor, MI, Servant Publications, 1993) p. 263.
4. Francis MacNutt, <u>Deliverance from Evil Spirits</u>, (Grand Rapids: Chosen Books, 1995) pp. 76-86.

5. Francis MacNutt, <u>Deliverance from Evil Spirits,</u> (Grand Rapids: Chosen Books, 1995) p. 212.

6. Francis MacNutt, <u>Deliverance from Evil Spirits,</u> (Grand Rapids: Chosen Books, 1995) pp. 215-216.

7. Jack Hayford, <u>The Power and Blessing</u>, (Wheaton: Victor Books, 1994) p. 103.

Section 7: Spiritual Warfare

1. Dean Sherman, <u>Spiritual Warfare For Every Christian,</u> (Seattle: YWAM Publishing, 1995) p. 141

2. Bill E. Billheimer, <u>Destined for the Throne,</u> (Minneapolis: Bethany House Publishers, 1975) pp. 19-27

3. Ibid, p. 17

4. Francis Frangipane, <u>The Three Battlegrounds,</u> (Cedar Rapids: Advancing Church Publications, 1989) p. 3.

5. Eugene H. Peterson, <u>The Message,</u> (Colorado Springs: NAVPRESS, 1993) p. 173.

6. Dean Sherman, <u>Spiritual Warfare for Every Christian,</u> (Seattle: YWAM Publishing, 1995) p. 28.

7. Items 1-5 have been adapted from Larry Lea, <u>The Weapons of Your Warfare,</u> (Lake Mary, Florida: Creation House, 1989) pp. 39-40

8. Derek Prince, <u>Blessing or Curse,</u> (Grand Rapids, Michigan: Chosen Books, 1990) pp. 42.

9. This section adapted from Francis Frangipane, <u>The Three Battlegrounds,</u> (N.P., Advancing Church Publications, 1989) pp. 6-8

10. Items 1-3 adapted from Ed Murphy, "We Are at War," C. P. Wagner and F. Douglas Pennoyer, ed., <u>Wrestling With Dark Angels,</u> (Ventura, Regal Books, 1990) pp. 49-72

11. Francis Frangipane, <u>The Three Battlegrounds,</u> (N.P.: Advancing Church Publications, 1989), p. 7.

12. Francis Frangipane, <u>The Three Battlegrounds,</u> (N.P.: Advancing Church Publications, 1989), p. 7

13. This section on the armor is adapted from Neil T. Anderson, <u>The Bondage Breaker,</u> (Eugene, Oregon: Harvest House Publishers, 1990), pp. 79-86.

14. Peter J. Moore, "Binding Prayer for Protection", (<u>Journal of Christian Healing</u>. Volume 12. No. 1, Spring 1990), p. 23.

15. Francis Frangipane, <u>The Three Battlegrounds,</u> (N.P.: Advancing Church Publications, 1989) p. 8.

16. This teaching on the Lord's prayer was adapted from a message by Pastor Bill Johnson, Bethel Church, Redding, CA. in 2002.

17. Judson Cornwall, Let Us Praise, (Plainfield, New Jersey: Logos International, 1973) p. 135

18. Michael D. Evans, "The Foolishness of God", (Bakersfield, CA: Bakersfield Christian Life Center, September 18, 1993.)

19. Watchman Nee, <u>The Body of Christ: a Reality,</u> (New York, Christian Fellowship Publishers, Inc., 1978).

Section 10: Generational Healing

1. (New Jerusalem Bible, 1985 by Darton, Longman and Todd. Doubleday & Co. Garden City, NY)

2. This teaching on Generational Healing was adapted from Christian Healing Ministries, School of Healing Prayer Level I Facilitators Manual. 1999, Jacksonville FL.

Appendix M:

1. Adapted from class notes prepared by John C. McClure, Pastor, Vineyard Christian Fellowship (Costa Mesa, CA) for a conference in Anaheim, CA on June 21, 1987.

Appendix N:

1   Adapted from class notes prepared by John C. McClure, Pastor, Vineyard Christian Fellowship (Costa Mesa, CA) for a conference in Anaheim, CA on June 21, 1987.

About Wholeness Ministries

Wholeness Ministries was founded in 1989 to help train and equip the Church to follow the Great Commission of Matthew 28:18-19 to go and "Do What Jesus Did." Jesus demonstrated the power of God in signs, wonders and miracles. Our Purpose and Mission is to pray for healing and train believers to effectively minister to those in need of physical healing, inner healing and deliverance ministry. Based on our understanding of Luke 4:18-19, we believe that God is calling us as never before to radical obedience. As we submit ourselves to Him, we are empowered to proclaim the Gospel and to demonstrate it under the anointing of the Holy Spirit. We are to do the works of His Kingdom: to release the oppressed, heal the sick and proclaim the Good News. Operating in unconditional love and the transforming power of God we, the "Children of the King," can demonstrate God's healing power by proclamation of the "Good News" and by praying for the sick. God is calling us as never before to bring His Kingdom to our families, homes, jobs, schools and communities.

We have never experienced the anointing and empowering of God's people as we are experiencing it now. We see throughout the church worldwide God drawing us into a place where we are to walk in radical obedience. He is calling us into relationship and intimacy that requires we spend significant time with Him in silence and solitude, listening to His heart, feeling what He feels, seeing what He sees. Then we are to go out into the marketplace where we work, shop, and live daily. In this marketplace we are to be Jesus to the world by doing what Jesus would do.

Wholeness Ministries offers training which helps individuals see by "hands on" demonstration, how to pray for others. We conduct training schools and offer individual prayer sessions at our offices in Bakersfield, CA. We are also available to conduct healing services, retreats, conferences and workshops on specific topics related to all areas of healing. In addition, we conduct seminars centered on Mike Evans' new book, "Why Not Waste Time With God," a book whose focus is to move us beyond a superficial relationship with God to live in intimacy with him.

We have ministered extensively in Northern Ireland, England, Puerto Rico, Hungary, Canada, India and extensively throughout the United States. To schedule a Wholeness Ministries conference, or to receive additional information, please contact us at:

P.O. Box 80503
Bakersfield, CA 93380 U.S.A.
Phone: (661) 833-2920
Fax: (661) 833-2934
E-Mail: mevans@wholeness.org
www.wholeness.org

What people are saying about

Learning to Do What Jesus Did

"I heartily recommend Mike Evans' manual on prayer ministry (Learning to do What Jesus Did). I know Mike personally and he is eminently practical, as well as being a sound, balanced teacher in the areas of both healing and deliverance. This book would be an excellent guide if you yourself want to learn how to pray for healing or, better yet to train a prayer team for your church."

Francis MacNutt, Ph.D., Founder, Christian Healing Ministries

"If you want to build a healing ministry in your church buy this book and follow the directions. Its all here, Scriptural, practical, personal. Mike is a sure guide-he knows it, does it and helps others do it too. God is using Mike among others to restore the healing ministry of Jesus to the whole church."

Don Williams, Ph.D. Author,
"Signs, Wonders and the Kingdom of God," "Jesus and Addiction."

What people are saying about

Why Not Waste Time with God

"With passion and precision Mike addresses the great need of the believer to spend time with...no, 'waste' time with God. He successfully engages the reader into the drama of the Father's pursuit of His children. I was especially moved by his insights on 'our belovedness'. I can't help but think that his revelation alone would draw multitudes into a place of deep intimacy with God. Caution: the fire of heaven is on this book!" photo

Bill Johnson, Senior Pastor, Bethel Church, Redding, CA

"'A French acrobat once climbed to the top of a skyscraper with his five year old son on his back. When they came down, someone asked the child, 'were you scared up there?' Surprised by the question, the boy replied, 'No, I wasn't. My daddy was holding me.'"

"If you want to have this lovely story become your personal experience, read Mike Evans' powerful book on the irreplaceable importance of 'holy loitering' with God."

Brennan Manning, Author,
"The Ragamuffin Gospel", "The Relentless Tenderness of Jesus",
"The Signature of Jesus", and "The Importance of Being Foolish".

How to Pray for Others with Tangible Results... the
Learning to Do What Jesus Did
Media Series

| Product #40 | **Prayer Team Ministry Training Book** |

In Learning To Do What Jesus Did, you will discover unique approaches to praying for others. You will find a step-by-step plan for experiencing the healing power of Jesus in your ministry. After reading this book you will feel a new sense of freedom in praying for others. You will see wonderful, dynamic results as God uses you in exciting new ways to do the things Jesus did. This book will arm you with new knowledge, tools and confidence in praying effectively for yourself and others. As you will discover, learning to pray effectively is learning to follow Jesus. Also available in Spanish and Korean.

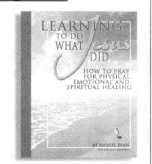

English Edition Book (Product #40) • $18.95 (plus shipping)
Spanish Edition Book • $18.95 (plus shipping)
Korean Edition Book • $18.95 (plus shipping)

| Product #41 | **9 DVD Series** |

This nine DVD video series is a must for pastors and lay ministers alike. It features approximately 10 hours of teaching from Michael and Jane Evans that will make ministering in the authority and power of Jesus easy to understand and exciting. Mike and Jane have taught this in many different denominations as well as several countries around the world. This series features the following DVD's:

1) Introduction to Healing
2) A Healing Model
3) The Role of Faith
4) Authority of the Believer
5) Introduction to Inner Healing
6) Biblical Examples of Inner Healing
7) Forgiveness and Inner Healing
8) Deliverance
9) Spiritual Warfare

English Edition available on 9 DVD's • $149 (plus shipping)
Spanish Edition available on 9 DVD's • $149 (plus shipping)

| Product #42 | **9 CD Series** |

This nine CD series contains an edited version of the Learning to Do What Jesus Did DVD Series (Product #41).

English Edition, 9 CD's • $59.95 (plus shipping)
Spanish Edition, 9 CD's • $59.95 (plus shipping)

To Order, Go To:
www.Wholeness.org

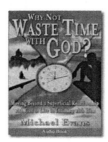

Walking Into a Life
of Healing and Wholeness

Product #43	Healing the Wounded Self-Image (3 CD's)

When you look at yourself in the mirror, what do you see? Do you like what you see? Satan's greatest psychological weapon is a gut-level feeling of inferiority, inadequacy, and low self-worth. This 3CD series will help you understand how to bring healing to these areas of your life. The topics covered are: Healing the Wounded Self-Image, Breaking Inner Vows and Restoring Your Spirit.

3 CD's • $24.95 (plus shipping)

Product #44	Our Authority to Break Curses and Soul Ties (1 CD)

People can be in bondage due to sin, soul ties and various types of curses, without knowledge of such bondage in their lives. In this teaching we will explore the variety of ways we come under the influence of these curses and soul ties, and will learn how we have been given authority through the Holy Spirit to break their influence over us.

1 CD • $6.00 (plus shipping)

Product #45	Traps of Unforgiveness (1 CD)

The key to freedom from bondage and growth and intimacy with God is found in forgiveness. Most of the ground Satan gains in the lives of Christians is due to unforgiveness. This teaching will reveal Satan's traps and how you can break free from them.

1 CD • $6.00 (plus shipping)

Product #46	The Father's Heart (3 CD's)

We know from Scripture we are Children of God. Often when He does try to speak to us we don't really want to hear what He has to say or we don't know for sure that it is God talking. Part of that is because we have barriers we've built that keep us from understanding the depth of intimacy with which our Father God loves us. This series helps remove the barriers to intimacy with the Father and live in the freedom and power of our identity in Christ.

3 CD's • $24.95 (plus shipping)

To Order, Go To:
www.Wholeness.org

Walking Into a Life
of Healing and Wholeness

Product #47	Understanding Your Authority (1 CD)

 When we understand Spiritual Authority, we will experience freedom in every part of our lives. It will happen when we recognize and use the gift of authority we have from God. We have this authority available to us today and we need to know how to operate in this authority.

1 CD • $6.00 (plus shipping)

Product #48	Going for the Gold or Going for the Furnace? (1 CD)

 What are you willing to die for? We all give our lives to something. It may be our job, family, wealth, status, drugs, sex, or material things. It is easy for these things to become idols and replace God in our lives. How do we identify and destroy them and put ourself back in the place where God is truly Lord over our lives.

1 CD • $6.00 (plus shipping)

Product #49	These Giants are Coming Down (1 CD)

 All of us have giants in our lives that strike fear into us, or they seem so huge we feel we will never overcome them. This exciting teaching brings into focus those qualities which can be inherent in our daily walk as believers, and which should characterize our response when we face those giants.

1 CD • $6.00 (plus shipping)

To Order, Go To:
www.Wholeness.org

CPSIA information can be obtained at www.ICGtesting.com
Printed in the USA
BVOW050131110413

317876BV00004B/5/P